EMBEDDING CAREERS IN THE CURRICULUM

A practical guide to inspire students and deliver exceptional careers education

Tom Corry

Embedding Careers in the Curriculum

This first edition published in 2025 by Trotman, an imprint of Trotman Indigo Publishing Ltd, 18e Charles Street, Bath BA1 1HX.

© Trotman Indigo Publishing Ltd 2025

Author: Tom Corry

British Library Cataloguing in Publication Data
A catalogue record for this book is available from the British Library.

Paperback ISBN 978-1-911724-77-3
eISBN 978-1911724-78-0

All rights reserved. This book is sold subject to the condition that it shall not, by way of trade or otherwise, be lent, resold, hired out or otherwise circulated without the publisher's prior written consent in any form of binding or cover other than that in which it is published and without a similar condition including this condition being imposed on the subsequent purchaser. No part of this publication may be reproduced, stored in a retrieval system or transmitted in any form or by any means, electronic and mechanical, photocopying, recording or otherwise without prior permission of Trotman Indigo Publishing.

Every effort has been made to trace copyright holders and to obtain their permission for the use of copyright material. The publisher apologises for any errors or omissions, and would be grateful to be notified of any corrections that should be incorporated in future editions of this book.

The authorised representative in the EEA is Easy Access System Europe Oü (EAS), Mustamäe tee 50, 10621 Tallinn, Estonia.

Printed and bound in the UK by 4Edge Ltd, Hockley, Essex.

 All details in this book were correct at the time of going to press. To keep up to date with all the latest news and updates and to access the online resources that accompany this book, use this QR code or visit www.trotman.co.uk/pages/embedding-careers-in-the-curriculum-resources

For Gem, Jack and Povs.

Contents

About the author . . . vii
Welcome . . . xi

Introduction . . . 1
The bay leaf . . . 7

PART I: EARLY YEARS AND PRIMARY . . . 9

1| Storytelling for career exploration . . . 13
2| Challenging career assumptions . . . 21
3| Making careers relevant in primary classrooms . . . 27
4| Curriculum review: Embedding careers . . . 35
5| Finding the "why": Connecting learning to careers . . . 45
6| Preparing for the next step: Transition to secondary . . . 57

PART II: SECONDARY . . . 65

7| Starting strong: Career foundations in secondary school . . . 69
8| Moving beyond "because I said so": Purposeful careers learning . . . 77
9| Why teach? Why learn? Careers and purpose . . . 87
10| Beyond exams: Defining the purpose of subjects . . . 97
11| Mapping your careers curriculum: Identifying strengths and gaps . . . 105
12| Working with parents: A partnership for career success . . . 119

PART III: PUTTING FRAMEWORKS INTO ACTION . . . 125

The journey continues . . . 139
Further reading and additional resources . . . 143

About the author

Passionate about empowering students for success in both life and work, **Tom Corry** serves as the Careers Leader for the Bourne Education Trust. He was awarded the CDI Careers Leader of the Year in 2023. With a background that spans from Teaching Assistant to Head of Department, he has cultivated a deep understanding of the education landscape. He is committed to instilling essential career skills and confidence in students, starting from the earliest stages of their education. By bridging the gap between education and industry, he aims to bring businesses and employers into schools, fostering a culture of aspiration, breaking stereotypes, and removing barriers to success.

It is the obvious which is so difficult to see most of the time. People say "It's as plain as the nose on your face." But how much of the nose on your face can you see, unless someone holds a mirror up to you?

Issac Asamov, I Robot

Welcome

When it comes to national guidance put in place for the implementation of careers education in schools, the Gatsby Benchmarks are, as it turns out, pretty damn good. For those who know me, it likely comes as no surprise that, of their eight pillars, there's one I see as the essential core for any school truly striving to do its best for its young people: Benchmark 4 – Linking Curriculum Learning to Careers.

Benchmark 4 remains, in my view, the linchpin. It's the only one that truly seeks to weave together the past, present, and future, offering students the chance to find their own meaning and inherent value in their education. It's what allows careers education to become part of the very fabric of mainstream schooling, not just an add-on or last-minute thought bolted onto the end. Giving students every opportunity to forge a brighter future for themselves. That's the very purpose of education, and Benchmark 4 sits right at its heart.

Initially proposed in 2014, trialled in 2015, and then widely adopted in 2018, the Gatsby Benchmarks have indeed come a long way. 2024 marked their 10-year review, a chance to reflect on the journey of the past decade and look ahead to the next. One phrase from that review really stuck with me, something I held onto tightly: "Every year, in every subject, every pupil." No other benchmark addresses as much contact time in such a specific and powerful manner. Think about it – a student has the potential to be exposed to around 4,500 hours of careers-related learning during secondary education. That's a phenomenal opportunity.

And the engagement has grown year on year since its introduction. Schools are increasingly weaving it into their development plans, dedicated roles are emerging to drive its delivery, and the levels of external support are on the rise. The delivery of Benchmark 4? It's a whole-school effort, demanding the involvement of every single member of staff. Unlike many of the other benchmarks, it simply cannot be effectively delivered by one person alone. It has to be everyone, in every lesson, every single year.

Now, as we move forward from that 10-year review, the landscape has shifted again with the publication of the statutory guidance for careers education in 2025. This new guidance doesn't just nod to the Gatsby Benchmarks; it's explicitly structured around them, further cementing their crucial role. And that phrase, "Every year, in every subject, every pupil"? The statutory guidance has only deepened that commitment, making it even clearer that this isn't just an aspiration but an expectation for all. It reinforces that every teacher, in every subject, should be showing students how what they are learning connects to the world of work and future opportunities.

It's time to ensure that not a single moment is lost, wasted, or squandered. We need to make every effort so that every year we graduate a confident and well-prepared cohort. Every subject must be working towards that same common objective: to equip students with the knowledge and the skills they need to carve out meaningful careers. And absolutely crucially, every single pupil must be included; no one can be left behind.

It's time to unlock potential, and this understanding of Benchmark 4, now even more firmly embedded in statutory guidance, is key.

Introduction

> A beginning is the time for taking the most delicate care that the balances are correct.
>
> Frank Herbert, *Dune*

Before we start, I feel like I should make a preemptive apology. There are some things in my life I am genuinely passionate about, and given the forum for it, I will share them loudly. To me there is nothing more important than levelling the playing field. Giving every young person the opportunity to enjoy success and happiness. It is very unlikely that a student's success and happiness is going to be the same as your success or happiness. For us, however, as teachers and those working in education, it is our responsibility to remember this and our privilege to empower and equip them to find their own paths.

Storytelling is a powerful tool; a lot of what we do as educators is telling stories. Exams rely on facts, textbooks are full of them, and so why do we need teachers? We are the storytellers, we breathe life into the sterility of the textbook. A good teacher will take learning out of text and bring it into the classroom; a great teacher will embed it into the world and sew it into the lives of their students. This is where integrating careers education into the curriculum comes into its own. If you can break the misconception that careers education is telling students about the jobs you know about, and instead use it to instil into them the skills and integrity it takes to follow a dream, then you have changed a life. They will become the authors of their own stories.

Throughout the course of this book, I sincerely hope that you come to the same conclusion as me: careers education is what education should be. It doesn't matter the subject or level of education you teach, you are a careers educator first and a subject teacher second. It shouldn't just be about subjects within a school; careers education is about future-proofing young people. That is what schools are. They are places, institutions, and locations where you can future-proof our students and give them all the skills they need to follow a journey that is true and authentic to them. That is why we are in schools: as teachers, careers leaders, senior leaders, support staff, admin staff – whoever you are in the school, that is why you're there. That is what we need to keep at the forefront of our minds.

The way I see it is that we are currently at a crossroads in education; a decision needs to be made. Either on the ground floor or somewhere with a more expensive view, as to what the purpose of our education system is. Are we maintaining the status quo established back in the heart of the Industrial Revolution? Whereby our students attend school to work towards academic success and to remain occupied while parents can go to work and keep the economy rolling. Or are we more than that? Are we providing students with the tools, resources and drive to sculpt their future careers into something they are truly passionate about? By the simple act of picking up this book, I can probably guess which category you fall into.

We are at a point in history where the world of work is evolving at a rapid rate, while the traditional model of education is largely unchanged. The need for students to be able to memorise and digest vast amounts of information and subject knowledge is becoming more and more outdated. Employers are increasingly stating that qualifications in the classic sense are of lesser significance than the candidate's interpersonal and transferable skills. If the education system is to remain relevant and meaningful, it needs to change. While we might not be able to change policy on an individual level, we can show our students that there is more to the school system than meets the eye.

This is not new information; reports from research papers and reports led by industry voices, much more learned than I, are all echoing the same thing. It's all about skills. It's all about preparing young people for an unknown future. For most that read this, particularly in education, it can feel daunting that what we are doing is inadequate or in need of overhaul. This is not the case. Within every school and every classroom, there is a wealth of knowledge and enrichment. It is about highlighting and empowering our staff to take the leap of faith and push their subjects to the limits.

Think back to what education and the world of work were like just 10 years ago (the beauty of this is that the following statement is true regardless of the year this is read). It's almost unrecognisable compared to what the reality is today. How quickly have smartphone and AI technologies developed, and how fast have they integrated into our lives? Take a moment to think about your first mobile phone, and what is currently in your pocket now. Personally, my first phone was a good old-fashioned "snake" phone. My careers education and my career prospects back then were vastly different from what the students that we are all supporting now are facing.

One thing that is becoming hugely apparent, from more and more local, national and international reports, is that less and less emphasis is being placed on the quantity or even the discipline of qualifications students are obtaining. In fact, in many cases the topics taught are largely arbitrary.

Introduction

This is not a particularly popular topic, especially to take into schools, but it is becoming the reality of the world we are living in. Take science, for example. There is literally a universe of topics to choose from. The depth and variety of those taught are more often limited by the time constraints of the timetable and national curriculums than by the importance of one scientific principle over another. One thing, however, is common throughout the entire subject: the appreciation for the scientific method, telling the story of the evolution (if you'll pardon the pun) and the growth of understanding of the world around us centralised on the importance of questioning and collaboration to solve problems and come to reasoned and logical conclusions.

The reality is that there is a theme to what employers are looking for in prospective employees. Qualifications are low priority for what they see in the next generation workforce; skills are high. They want to see students with transferable skills; they want to find not just the best-qualified person for the job but the right person for the job. They want well-rounded individuals who have skills they can then utilise, develop, train, and progress.

Now, when you are taking this into schools and speaking with head teachers, senior leaders, and, in particular, the head of outcomes, it will not be an easy pill to swallow. The idea that traditional qualifications aren't the priority anymore is difficult for many in education. Qualifications open doors, absolutely, but more and more voices are calling for skills. These are the most useful attributes for young people to qualify with and take forward with them. If we're not supporting that in an educational setting, we're not doing those young people justice.

While the sell might be tough, the implementation is largely arbitrary. In fact, a large amount of the infrastructure is already in place. Teachers are the heart of the school; they are on the front line delivering their curriculums to students on a daily basis. The challenge comes with the shift of focus; the delivery of the knowledge is there, and now it is time to show the students why – why subject theory ties to their futures so much more than they realise.

You will have certainly heard, and let's face it, you have probably said yourself, "yeah, but, Miss, when am I ever going to need to know this in life?" It can be the kiss of death to a skillfully planned lesson for some. To me though, it is the start of the most important lesson I will have delivered that day. This is the opportunity to show students the reason why they are in school, in a classroom, with a real-life teacher and not learning from a textbook in isolation. It is a chance to ignite their passions and sell the all-important bigger picture at play.

This is where this book falls; it straddles the line between a rigorous curriculum and unabridged chaos. If you are anything like me, and I would suspect you are, you are in the classroom day in day out, not because you have the determination to follow a regimented curriculum at any cost. But because you see the potential inside each and every student, and you will do your damnedest to draw it out.

There are three assumptions that I will make throughout this book; they are, I hope, assumptions that you will share with me. Or at the very least, understand why they have been made.

1. **Teachers work hard!**

    The last thing this book should lead to is anyone working any harder than they already are. It should not result in a new initiative to be launched during a conference day at the start of the academic year and should not become onerous on people to the extent that careers education becomes resented in your school. Building a meaningful careers programme with a lasting legacy should not rely on protocols to be followed by staff. It should also avoid a regimented, dictated approach that is consistently taught in every single lesson, as this simply isn't practical. For the same reason that there is no "right" career path to follow, there is no "right" way for teachers to approach it in their curriculums and lessons. The most significant factor is that staff are well informed, supported, and empowered to guide their students. They should educate them not only on the knowledge and content of their subject but also on the significance it will play in their lives.

    There is a reason why this is the first assumption I have chosen to talk about. It is, by far, the most important and one that should be kept at the forefront of your mind: teachers work hard. Careers education should augment everything that we do as educators whenever we interact with students. It can be explicit, implicit, or something in between. But it needs to be fully immersive and when it works well, it costs us no more time or effort; it simply becomes part of our everyday practice.

2. **There are pockets of genius unique to you and your school already.**

    Every single school is unique. There are, of course, similarities between schools. But these are institutions consisting of hundreds of individuals of all ages; hundreds of lives all crossing past each other and interacting in unique ways every single day. There will be moments of wonder being realised in all kinds of places. Find these moments and capitalise on them; these will become your starting point and will often form the heart of your careers programme from which everything else stems or rallies around.

    It is worth remembering that some of the best practices may not be taking place within the classroom. It may be with the student pastoral support teams; it may be within the Special Educational Needs and Disabilities (SEND) or safeguarding departments; it could be within the premises teams or with recurring engagements with external partners. It is worth dedicating a proportion of your time to investigating and auditing these avenues as they will pay off and start to connect the dots that make your school setting unique. This can't be done from inside an office or behind a desk; you will need to get out and speak to people. Spend time in the staffroom having a chat; if you see a member of staff outside with students at lunch, go join them; hang out in the canteen and get to know the catering staff. You don't know where to look until you have found it.

3. **Careers education is more than just advertising a list of jobs to students.**
   This might seem like an obvious point, but it can be surprising how often the misconception appears. Careers education is about telling students what jobs exist at the moment, or more often, what jobs existed in the past. While there is an absolute need to inform students of the current labour market, what guarantee is there that the jobs available to work today will be there when they join the world of work? Odds are, they simply won't.

   Speaking of jobs, the world of work is evolving at a rapid pace; to tell a student that they would suit a particular job or company is at best uninspiring and at worst career limiting. Words spoken by teachers hold power, regardless of how much they think they are listened to at the time. Students will hold onto them for the rest of their lives. It is important to support teachers to ensure that they are in a position to guide and inspire students to follow their own paths and make informed decisions about what their careers might look like.

   How many stories have you been told of the past experiences of people's interactions with careers advisers? They boast of the inaccuracy of their suggested career paths. I get this on an almost weekly basis, and I even joke that I never did become a highways maintenance patrol officer, but this is by the by. The point is that pointing outright the "right" career for a student is a sure-fire way to get it wrong.

When it comes to young people and education, repetition is key. For learning to stick, there must be recall and reapplication. You know what, get rid of "young people" and replace it with "everyone". For the overwhelming majority of us, learning something new, be it a physical skill, a mental skill, or simply the recalling of information, requires consistency, repetition, and time. In education we have capacity for all three. We have 12 captive years with a student through primary and secondary education, and it is time to do more than just get them a GCSE. It's time to show them what they are capable of.

The purpose of this book is to equip you, your staff, and your students with the tools and resources needed to develop a curriculum that truly prepares young people for a fulfilling and lasting career journey. Each chapter addresses a common and current challenge within our educational landscape, offering a fresh perspective along the way. To support quick access to key ideas, you'll find introductory **Summary Points** and a concluding **Action Checklist** in every chapter. Additionally, each chapter features a practical toolkit aligned with its theme, either an **In-Class Resource** for immediate use or a **Staff Support Resource** to help you empower colleagues. Finally, there is a a range of useful **Online Resources** that accompany this book, which can be accessed by scanning the QR code or visiting the web address at the start of this book.

Careers education is a broad, interconnected field that relies on the engagement of multiple stakeholders to make a meaningful impact. This book explores these dimensions throughout. For example, parental involvement is addressed in Chapter 12 – *Working with parents: A partnership for career success* and Chapter 8 – *Moving beyond "because I said so": Purposeful careers learning*. Curriculum audits at both primary and secondary levels are tackled in Chapter 4 – *Curriculum review: Embedding careers* and Chapter 11 – *Mapping your careers curriculum: Identifying strengths and gaps*. Staff training and the mindset shift needed to integrate careers meaningfully are central to Chapter 9 – *Why teach? Why learn? Careers and purpose* and Chapter 10 – *Beyond exams: Defining the purpose of subjects*.

While these themes are organised by topic, the heart of this book remains firmly student-centred. Every chapter ultimately circles back to their needs, ambitions, and futures.

The bay leaf

> We stand against the small tide of those who want to make everyone unhappy with conflicting theory and thought.
> Ray Bradbury, *Fahrenheit 451*

Everyone has a lens through which they see the world: a philosophy, point of view, doctrine, ideology; whatever you want to call it. In some cases, this is a simple idea or thought; it doesn't go much further than that. For others it begins to take hold and take over in such a way that it becomes all-encompassing and their primary outlook. Referring to a bay leaf as a philosophy is odd, but for me, I'll grant you that it works. In particular, it works in the context of education and how it engages with the fourth industrial revolution. Let me explain.

The bay leaf is a mysterious character, very unassuming; it isn't particularly large, like a lily plant, it isn't intriguingly small, like the thyme. It doesn't have the vibrance of a maple, the wonder of a cheese plant or the sharp intensity of mint. If you were to ask a child to draw you a leaf, the odds are it would resemble a bay leaf. It is simple and, for all intents and purposes, just a leaf. This is not to say it isn't special and exciting in its own right. But for it to come into its own and shine, it must be part of something bigger, something greater than the sum of its parts. The bay leaf is the epitome of where careers education sits in the stew of a student's education.

The solution I am proposing to the crisis we are facing in education isn't, to continue the metaphor, to make a new meal or to redesign the menu. It is largely inevitable that the system will continue in its current guise for many years, certainly from an individual school level. Instead, we can enrich and interweave a new narrative into our everyday practice, a story we have known for a long time. Students need to know that what they are learning reaches far beyond the curriculum and holds a deeper meaning than learning for learning's sake. We need to drop the bay leaf into the casserole of education.

Now you can take this analogy as far as you want; you can speculate on the representations of different meats and vegetables and how they relate to the education of young people. For me though, it is enough to know that school, as a concept, at its core, is fine; it's perfunctory. Sometimes you get moments of greatness, but on the whole, it is lacking true depth and meaning. Something more is needed to spice it up a bit and give it some richness. Something that is ever present and lends its flavour to every corner of the school, enriching everything it touches.

Introducing an integrated, skills and student-centred careers programme into the curriculum is where the mundane and normal become inspiring and exceptional. This is the intention of the following chapters. Starting at the start with students as they enter education is crucial, and maintaining consistency throughout their school journeys will enable them to see the bigger picture sooner rather than later, thus enabling them to keep open minds and prepare them for a world which is not yet ready for them.

If you have made it this far, then you are probably in agreement on where our educational system sits in society. We are torn between the pull of exam boards and rigid curriculums on one side, and onerous inspections and elitist results tables on the other. You are filled with a drive to inspire a new generation to fulfil their potential, yet equally see the benefit of a rounded education on the other. That, or you are humouring me. Either way, it would be really great if you would continue further. It is very easy for someone to tell you something is broken; it is harder to be convinced, and harder still to suppose a solution.

I will therefore finish this section with something of an apology. I am not an academic researcher and I am not a highly qualified practitioner. I am someone who, much like yourself, maybe, has walked the path and seen that it's not all that it should be or indeed could be. Something isn't right with our educational system, and this is how I propose we begin to change it – with one teacher, with one lesson, one day at a time.

PART I
Early years and primary

> You start a question, and it's like starting a stone. You sit quietly on the top of a hill; and away the stone goes, starting others...
> Robert Louis Stevenson, *The Strange Case of Dr. Jekyll and Mr. Hyde*

Careers education starts from the moment you begin to learn. This isn't to say that you are thinking about what job you want to do while you are taking your first steps, but you are certainly starting to form your impressions of the world and your sense of self. There is a lot of psycho-developmental science at play here; this is not the place for it, nor is this the medium to suppose it. Suffice to say that learning has begun and, therefore, so must the integration of careers learning.

As previously established, teachers work hard, and nowhere is this more evident than in primary classrooms. Lessons are constantly adapted, differentiated, restructured, or even restarted, all on the turn of a hat. They are wildly dynamic and vibrant, with input from multiple directions and sources and a chaotic love of learning from the students. At the centre of it all is the classroom teacher, orchestrating it with an artful control.

Primary schools might seem like the last place to be raising the topic of careers learning, particularly with four-to-five-year-olds in pre-Key Stage year groups. But it is at these ages when students are at their most receptive; habits and opinions formed at this stage will go on to inform the next day, then week, then year, then decades of their education. While every single day might not be remembered, their experience and learning almost certainly will be and will form a significant part of their personal and professional outlook.

Primary schools are the educational settings which set the foundations and expectations for a student's future, equipping them with the readiness and preparedness to take learning with them into life and be open to new experiences. Their path through school from Early Years and Year 1 to 6 sees them go through more changes and experiences than at any other stage of their education; to say they are the formative years would be a colossal understatement. Throughout this time students are guided through all aspects of growing up and sowing the seeds for their potential for future growth and development. With schools being the stepping stones into adulthood and the world of work, why is it that careers-related learning is so often put to the wayside, or relegated to a single day or week of the year for select year groups?

Understanding primary careers education holds significant implications for educators across all phases. The foundations of career-related attitudes, skills, and aspirations are undeniably laid within these formative years. For secondary school staff, understanding this groundwork is paramount. It enables them to build more effectively upon students' existing capabilities, address any misconceptions or stereotypes that may have begun to take root, and collaborate with primary colleagues to ensure a cohesive and progressive careers education journey for each student. Therefore, this section is not simply a guide for primary practitioners but a vital resource for anyone committed to supporting students' long-term success in acquiring these crucial skills.

One of the first lessons students begin to learn during their induction into education isn't how to read, write, or do maths; it isn't how to analyse information and apply it for examination purposes. The first lessons that are learnt revolve around independence, meeting and communicating with new people, and understanding the importance of cooperation and sharing. These are all basic lessons, which are not assessed or graded on a curve, but they are instilled into them as they begin to form their relationships with school, teachers and peers.

Speak to any primary teacher and ask them what they do with regard to careers education with their students. They will likely respond with either "Nothing at all, this is primary school, it's not in our curriculum" or they will tell you that they "have events throughout the year where parents or local uniformed service and business people come in to speak to students about their jobs". One thing is for certain: they are completely underestimating themselves. Remember that careers education is more than job advertisement; it is about providing all young people with the skills and qualities they need to become successful and have agency in their lives and careers.

This is why careers education is so key to get in early, but also to get it right early. This is the ideal moment to start highlighting and encouraging all of those nuggets of extra learning and enrichment that a well-structured curriculum delivers; this is the moment to start thinking about what journey you want your students to take on throughout school and what foundations need to be set to support this.

At this point, it should be made clear that the majority of an outstanding careers programme will already be in place. Much like with the Early Years programme, it is about redefining and realigning the curriculum to enhance and shine a light on what is there, not build on it for building sake. There is no sure-fire way to ensure a school-wide programme fails than by trying to redesign the wheel. While integrating a careers programme should not be the cause for a redesign, it should absolutely be part of one when it occurs.

Students in this phase of education are open to new ideas and are primed to be receptive to alternative ways of thinking. Adults, on the other hand, are much more likely to be hesitant when approached with new ideas and will need support to rethink their approach to teaching and education in general.

Ultimately, recognising and nurturing the seeds of careers learning within primary education is not about pushing young children towards specific jobs. Instead, it is about cultivating the essential skills, attitudes, and awareness that will empower them to navigate their future lives and careers with confidence and agency. The following chapters will explore how this crucial foundation is built and how it can be further strengthened.

1 | Storytelling for career exploration

Summary points

Integrating Career Awareness into Early Years Storytelling

By subtly shifting the way stories are read and discussed, teachers can introduce a foundation of career awareness, helping young learners make connections between storytelling and real-world roles.

Using Pre- and Post-Reading Questions to Enhance Engagement and Learning

Thoughtfully designed questions before and after reading can deepen comprehension, spark curiosity, and encourage children to think beyond the story, fostering both critical thinking and personal connections.

Developing Questioning Strategies to Support Critical Thinking and Comprehension

Creating dynamic and open-ended questions allows students to explore stories more deeply, enhancing their ability to predict, analyse, and reflect on key themes and ideas.

It is important to note that within the Early Years classroom, there is a huge amount of enriching and powerful work being delivered on a daily basis with a careers learning focus. This isn't about rewriting or developing whole schemes of work; it is about shifting perspective and highlighting what once was not so obvious. Then bringing to the surface the additional layers of learning which, until this point, may well have remained subliminal or unspoken.

Learning point

Within the Early Years framework, there is a series of objectives or statements that relate to the reading, or the guided listening to, of stories led by an adult. As a single statement or objective, this is very straightforward; it serves a very real purpose, but as a programme of learning, it doesn't expose any learning that is necessarily outside of its own context.

> Shifting the focus of delivery and introducing a slight change to the structure of this task not only fulfils its purpose within the curriculum. It also begins to lay the foundations of career awareness with students and extends the learning from the abstract into the realm of careers education.
>
> Discussions before and after the reading of a story add an entirely new dimension to the activity.
>
> **Pre-reading**
>
> - What do you think this story will be about? Based on the title, the cover pictures, and any other information to hand, what do you think will happen?
>
> - What do you think the characters will be like? Will they be helpful, happy, rude, funny?

These questions will start to engage students in thinking about the world beyond their current understanding and their own lives. It also encourages prediction and evaluation methods of thinking within a specific context. A context that is outside of their usual areas of learning where these skills would be used.

> This is then bookended with a similar collection of questions that tie the activity up in such a way as to prime them to remember and recall information in a new way, all the while keeping careers- or job-related thinking towards the forefront.
>
> **Post-reading**
>
> - What do you think the characters were doing before the story started?
>
> - What do you think the characters will do now that the story has finished?
>
> - What do you think the characters do for jobs? Have they always had that job? Will they always do it?
>
> The first two of these questions are all about engaging imagination and visualisation within a specific area: asking students to think of all stories, such as the lives of people around them as well as the non-fictional texts in discussion. This sets the learning in a place which can be, for all intents and purposes, in the real world, thereby allowing students to empathise with the characters on a level set in curiosity.

> With both these activity extensions, selecting the right text is important, while it can be applied to virtually any story or fable, and making the leap to the real world might not be practical or, indeed, logical. The right text can be used to guide independent learning activities at other points during the day. With it being further developed by bridging it to the next point. Therefore, encouraging students to engage with self-guided learning during role-play opportunities or adult-led learning tasks.

This approach to tweaking the lesson structure or planning is where the bayleaf approach truly shines. It requires minimal additional work or preparation. To be most effective, the line of questioning should be dynamic and responsive to the flow of the lesson, naturally emerging at different moments within the activities. Pre-planning a set of regimented questions that will be asked is largely pointless and likely to be ineffective. It will come across as forced and quickly lose the interest of the students. Instead, treating it as a conversation and, as with a conversation, taking into account the rhythm and points of interest is what will make it natural and seamless in how it is received and engaged with.

By letting staff, and by action, students, build this into their classrooms over time, it sets a firm foundation beyond curriculum discussions. Introducing exploration which can evolve and develop with the building confidence of the staff. In addition to this, it's important to note that, just as pre-planning regimented lessons can be ineffective, forcing this approach into every moment of every lesson can also be counterproductive. It risks undermining the natural and dynamic qualities that make this type of activity most effective.

IN-CLASS RESOURCE

Example questions from some classic genres to help you along the way.

Pre-reading questions

Fairy Tales:

The one about the porky triplets just trying to build a home

- What do you know about this story already?
- How else could this story end? What would be unusual?
- What different things could you build houses out of? Which ones would be best and why?

Everyday Life/Routines:

The one about the mummy elephant who wants some quiet time

- Why might someone want to have some quiet time alone?
- Have you ever wanted some time alone?
- Why do you think it is important for people to have quiet time?

Nature and Seasons:

The one about the insect that eats its way through a wonderful buffet

- How does what you eat make you feel?
- What foods make you think of the summer/winter?
- Why do you think the caterpillar needs to eat? What do caterpillars turn into?

Adventure:

The one about the family that goes out looking for a bear

- What makes something an adventure?
- What do you need to do to have an adventure?
- What should you do to prepare for an adventure?

Post-reading questions

Fairy Tales:

The one about the porky triplets just trying to build a home

- If they were real-life adults, what would you call their jobs?
- Which one would you most want to build you a new house? Why?
- What if the wolf was actually trying to help the pigs build better houses?

Everyday Life/Routines:

The one about the mummy elephant who wants some quiet time

- How could you help someone in your life have some quiet time?
- Do you think the mummy was happy at the end of the book?
- Do you think the mummy would be happier or less happy if she had peace and quiet from the start?

1| Storytelling for Career Exploration

Nature and Seasons:

The one about the insect that eats it way through a wonderful buffet

- Where do you think it found all of the food?
- Who made all of the food that was eaten?
- How do you think it made them feel when it was all gone?

Adventure:

The one about the family that goes out looking for a bear

- Why do you think the family took risks during their adventure?
- What do you think they learnt during their journey?
- Do you think they will do it again?

STAFF SUPPORT RESOURCE

A few pointers on where and how to start writing careers-focused comprehension questions.

Creating pre-reading questions

Activate prior knowledge

- Relate to similar themes or knowledge students have recently acquired.
- Establish lessons learnt from other situations such as home or other life experiences.

Spark curiosity

- Help students "want" to learn especially about things that they find new and interesting.
- Build and instil an awareness of anticipation and appreciate the imaginative thought processes it creates.

Predict events

- Support students in making predictions based on prior knowledge and interests.
- Encourage students to collect evidence to make informed predictions about the future.

Introduce key vocabulary

- Re-expose students to new vocabulary introduced in the story.
- Encourage students to use the vocabulary or language from the story in their discussions.

Creating post-reading questions

Check comprehension

- The most common use for questions after the fact of delivery is to see how much the students took in and can articulate.
- It is a very basic approach.

Encourage critical thinking

- Pose questions that don't necessarily have simple and straightforward answers; encourage them to make one to two logical steps to reach a conclusion.
- Allow students time to respond to dialogue and engage in a back-and-forth conversation with you.

Make personal connections to the story and characters

- Pose questions that allow students to place themselves into the stories or characters, building empathy and imaginative play.
- Encourage students to imagine themselves in different situations which might be unfamiliar to their everyday experience, then pose questions that motivate them to think about their actions and reactions within it.

Re enforce moral or thematic lessons

- What is the difference between right and wrong, good and bad, happy and sad? How do the characters demonstrate this, and how are these concepts demonstrated in the classroom?
- Allow students to explore how different moral themes might make them feel if they were in the particular situations that the characters found themselves in.

Tips for writing and preparing questions

- Generate a list of generic questions and create a list of variations which can be easily adapted.
  - "What happened in the story?"
    - What happened that you didn't expect?
    - What happened that you did expect?
    - What was your favourite/least favourite moment in the story?
    - Why did the characters behave the way they did?

- "Did the story end as you thought it would?"
  - How would you have changed the ending if you had the chance?
  - How would you react if you were in the story?
  - Was this story like real life or make-believe? Why do you think that?

Remember:

- Keep questions open.
- Avoid questions which have objectively correct answers.
- Visually back up questions using illustrations from the book or props to hold onto.
- Introduce new language sooner rather than later.
- Prize justified opinions over correct answers, every day of the week.

Action checklist

- ☑ Create a bank of "pre-reading" and "post-reading" questions (use the examples as your starting point). Focus on questions that go beyond basic comprehension to spark prediction, character analysis, and real-world connections.

  Think: action-oriented questioning.

- ☑ Experiment with open-ended questions like "What if...?", "Why do you think...?", and "How could this be different?" Resist the urge for simple "yes/no" questions. Focus on conversation flow and responding to student cues, not just sticking to a script.

  Think: conversation-led learning, not script-led questions.

- ☑ Take a moment to reflect. Did you feel comfortable moving away from fact-based questions? How did the children respond to the more open-ended approach? Identify one small tweak you could make to your questioning style for the next session to make it even more natural and effective.

  Think: continuous improvement, one question at a time.

2 | Challenging career assumptions

Summary points

Identifying and Addressing Stereotypes in Early Years Education

Stereotypes can subtly influence children's understanding of the world, making it crucial for teachers to recognise and challenge them before they become ingrained in their learning and play.

Using Storytelling and Discussion to Promote Inclusive Thinking

By carefully selecting and framing stories, teachers can guide discussions that encourage children to question stereotypes, explore diverse perspectives, and develop a more inclusive worldview.

Enhancing Role-Play and Activities to Reflect Diverse Careers and Histories

Integrating career-based role-play and historical exploration helps children connect past and present professions, broadening aspirations and beginning to form an understanding of the evolving world of work.

It can be exceedingly easy, and largely unintentional, to introduce stereotypes, particularly with young learners. While this may seem harmless, and often is in the short term, if left unchallenged or unaddressed by role models within their lives, it can become a repeated pattern. Over time, these habits may take root throughout a student's education, ultimately shaping behaviours that are likely to impact their future career paths. Cutting off access to paths that they may have never considered.

Author's note

There are a lot of classic children's stories which propagate these stereotypes. That isn't to say that these are inappropriate to use, but care should be taken to remind students that the roles of the characters within it are not defined by gender, race, or any other characteristic which could lead to stereotyping. This doesn't mean that every single text needs to be so wrapped up in this that it loses all meaning or interest. It can be a tricky path to tread, especially with there being such a wide variety of available stories to choose from, just keep variety and representation at the forefront of your mind and you can't go far wrong.

Addressing these head-on during these formative years is crucial; there will be a lot of moments where students will be engaging in self-directed learning, through imagination and role-play. While this is fundamental for development, it can also act as an echo chamber for these stereotypes. This is also addressed in the Early Years Foundation Stages (EYFS) Statutory Framework (2024), specifically regarding the Early Learning Goals within Understanding the World.

 Learning point

Two Early Learning Goals state that students should be able "to know some of the similarities and differences of things in the past and now" as well as "talk about the lives of people around them". Both of these statements can be easily addressed through storytelling, guided research or even through a school trip. But without context or guidance, stereotypes can be compounded through the independent play following this.

Neither of these Early Learning Goals in themselves directly address this, nor should they; this is not their purpose. However, it is important that teachers are aware that following these goals verbatim as they are stated can lead to the establishment of self, or peer, derived fixed mindsets in students, that once set, become significantly harder to break.

Delivering a "show and tell" task focused on the theme of the past and present of the people around them may involve asking students to bring in an object or photograph related to their family's history and their current family life and speak about it to their peers. This creates a fantastic opportunity to explore a multitude of themes and ideas, leading to rich learning and meaningful discussion.

 Learning point

You ask students to bring in a photograph of an adult in their family from the past and from now, and talk about who they are and how they have changed. The students who are taking part all complete their duties and there might be some questions asked of them, and possibly some answers given. No doubt students will take pride in this task and relish the moment to speak about something that is important to them.

This is a lovely way to work towards the related Early Learning Goals; however, they are sitting on a potential goldmine of further inquiry, enrichment, and inclusion if there was a slight tweak put in place at point of planning.

Rather than asking students to bring in a generic photograph, ask them to bring in a photograph or object of someone in their family's past that reflects the job they had. Ask them to find out/tell their peers about this job. This can be followed up with a discussion rather than a line of questioning, around the type of job they carried out, what they thought it may have been like to do, as well as think about how it relates to today's jobs being carried out for people in the present.

Shifting the focus onto the careers of the past doesn't change the fact that the Early Learning Goals are still being met. In addition to this, students are in a position where they can start to make personal links from artefacts from their past and family history with themselves. Activities like this allow students to start to find their own place in the world, make connections with their past and begin to visualise their future.

This alternative approach not only supports the students' development and stretches the learning into the realm of careers education. It also creates a task that is far more inclusive of students whose home situations may not be typical. By focusing instead on artefacts or sources that relate to a broader theme within the community such as work, volunteering, skills or hobbies, it will ensure that every student has the opportunity to contribute and feel involved regardless of their family structure or situation.

IN-CLASS RESOURCE

A series of resources to support students in exploration job roles and careers of the past and their links to modern day.

Who am I?

As a teacher, take on the role of a well-known job, asking the students to see if they can work out who you are and what you do for a living. This can be done by acting out different tasks or making comments which give them clues. This is then extended by encouraging them to ask you questions about you and your work. Activities like this always benefit from adding humour and embellishing the character you take on, making it as different as possible from your usual persona.

Give students the opportunity to have a go at it themselves. If they are more confident, they can carry this out in front of everyone, or set them into smaller groups to see if they can guess each other. Providing role-play equipment and clothing as well to give tangibility and support those who need a little inspiration.

With activities like this, students (and staff) will naturally fall into comfort zones. To begin with this is good, it means that they will begin to build confidence in the activity. However, this is all about breaking out of those comfort zones; tasking students to adopt roles they would otherwise be inclined to avoid having explored their own choice first then becomes a natural transition.

Jobs from the past

Set up role-play areas around the room that focus on particular jobs from the past, where students have the opportunity to explore them by physically acting them out. This is especially effective if tasked with identifying what the job might be called, what they did for a living, and if it still exists/what the modern equivalent is. Examples include:

- Blacksmith: providing students with basic tools to pretend to hammer horseshoes or other suitable objects, as well as protective equipment like gloves and aprons. Encourage them to think about how easy it might have been to do this job, and what skills they might have needed to have/use.
- Office worker/typist: making use of an old typewriter (supervision might be needed for this one), showing students how documents would have been created compared to using computers now. What would it have been like if you made a mistake?

- Farmer: provide students with small planting pots with seed; what do they need to grow? How would you do this for a whole sack of seeds and make sure they all grow?
- Train conductor: provide train tickets and a small hole punch for ticket punching, recreate a train environment, through chairs, or toys. This is a good opportunity for the students to continue their roles from other role-play areas by taking the train. In discussions, ask what train conductors do now. What technologies do they use and why?
- Baker/cook: well, this just depends how messy you want to get really.

Timelining

Run a washing line of string across the room to create an interactive timeline where students sort images or objects into a chronological order based on the evidence before them. Ask them to justify their choices and compare ideas as they do. What makes something more set in the past than something else? Once the order is set, discussions can begin around why there have been changes over time, what caused them, and what impact they think this has had on the world?

For a greater factor of integration, this activity can be used as part of most other topics that are being covered, thus seeding the fact that jobs and careers are applicable regardless of the context taught. For example:

The big three:

- Police uniforms: from the early peelers to modern police officers and detectives. How have their uniforms changed? What else has changed in terms of resources available to them?
- Firefighters: from the early firefighters of the late 1600s (post Great Fire of London) through to the vast array of modern firefighting equipment, and the additional roles they have taken on beyond firefighting.
- Healthcare professionals: from, well, whenever is suitable, some of the history of this can be quite gory, probably Florence Nightingale as a good starting point, depending on the age group of students you may take this further back to the Black Death and the Plague doctors who treated them.

> Innovation and invention:
>
> - Motor vehicles: from the original "horseless carriages" of the mid-1800s through to modern-day electric and hybrid vehicles. This might even be started from horse and carriage and include bicycles, depending on the topic being covered.
> - Planes and aviation: from the early hot air balloons, through to the Wright brothers and modern airliners and spacecraft, with the option to look forward to electric and autonomous vehicles.
>
> Toys and hobbies:
>
> - Children's toys: from early wooden toys to the introduction of fabrics, metals, and finally plastics, to be continued into the introduction of microchips and technological integrations.
> - Football and other sports: from the early sports kits and physical fitness of those who played, to the modern high-performance athletes and technologies that accompany it.

Action checklist

- ☑ Actively observe your learning environment, books, toys, displays, role-play areas. Identify any areas where gender, race, or other stereotypes might be unintentionally reinforced.
  Think: environmental audit for inclusivity.

- ☑ Review your go-to storybooks. Select one or two classic stories that might contain outdated stereotypes (even unintentionally). Plan to read these stories *intentionally*, prompting discussions that challenge those stereotypes. Use questions like, "Could the characters have different jobs?", "Do boys/girls always have to be like this in stories?".
  Think: proactive stereotype challenging through familiar texts.

- ☑ Audit your role-play areas. Are they reflecting a diverse range of careers and histories? Introduce new props, clothing, and scenarios that explicitly challenge stereotypes and showcase a wider world of work. Consider roles from the past and present, and consciously include representation.
  Think: role-play areas as stereotype-smashing zones.

3 | Making careers relevant in primary classrooms

Summary points

Embedding Careers Learning into Everyday Lessons

Rather than isolating careers education into stand-alone events, integrating it into regular lessons helps students make meaningful connections between their learning and the world beyond the classroom.

Maximising Impact while Minimising Teacher Workload

A successful careers programme should build on existing lesson plans, distributing the effort across subjects to avoid overwhelming staff while still ensuring students gain valuable insights into their futures.

Thematic Approaches to Careers Education

Using school-wide themes such as Net Zero, World Book Day, or Healthy Eating Week allows careers learning to blend seamlessly through various subjects, building curiosity and real-world connections into education.

Treading the lines between fostering curiosity, instilling a love of learning, establishing a baseline of working knowledge and developing students' sense of self is no mean feat. It's actually quite a lot to do. Tackling each one on its own as a stand-alone objective is a guaranteed way for anyone to put themselves into a gentle rock in the corner of a classroom. Instead, lessons are structured with a single, sometimes double, focal point in mind which will incorporate elements of all of the above, and more. Just because it is a phonics lesson, it doesn't mean that this is the only lesson which will be learnt. Within it there will be elements of self-discovery, guided learning, and personal development. This too is the process by which careers-related learning seeds itself into the primary classroom.

Careers learning will very rarely be the central focus of a lesson; this is fine, in fact, this is ideal. Much in the same way that trying to plan explicit examples of each point of student development that exists outside of the curriculum, planning an overt careers programme in this setting is a very good way to turn students away from the subject.

Embedding Careers in the Curriculum

> **Learning point**
>
> A school priority this year is around net zero and sustainability. It has been suggested by the leadership team that this would work really nicely with a careers focus. Specifically around showing students the problems we are currently facing and the jobs that are out there trying to fix it. The decision has been made to dedicate an afternoon to this, during which all normal lessons are suspended. Students will complete a bespoke lesson based on the theme, and there might even be some special guests invited to speak with them.
>
> The Science lead has been asked to produce activities for each of the year groups that can be delivered in this time. The emphasis is placed on the importance of sustainability for society and how it might relate to school life and the jobs that contribute to this sector.
>
> Diligently, they produce these resources for each class, with the outline of a lesson completed for them and the opportunity for teachers to make adjustments that they see fit for their classes. It goes really well, student feedback is very positive, they are able to articulate the importance of sustainability and net zero. Some students are even showing an interest in the careers and jobs relating to this and seeking to find out more.

On the surface, this initiative looks great; it is ticking all the right boxes. It's raising awareness of current affairs; showing students about jobs or careers they might not have heard about and providing them with a call to action which will almost certainly raise aspirations and begin to break down some stereotypes.

> However, the Science lead has put a huge amount of effort and time into producing these resources, "not a problem" they say, as it was a stand-alone event. Until its success sparks discussion around STEM careers for Space week or Engineering and Construction or Science week. All of a sudden, the realisation dawns that the majority of celebration weeks hold science, or more accurately STEM, at their heart.

Practically, one of these events is very achievable, but throw more into the mix and ironically (probably) it becomes unsustainable. Dig a little deeper, and cracks begin to show. For one, this is a lot of work for teachers to prepare for. It is not standard to their curriculum; it is bespoke. Therefore it is highly unlikely that they will not have historic resources or experience to pull from to support this as they usually would. It is also replacing standard lesson time, which will need to be recouped or consolidated at a later point, impacting planning again. The majority of staff will also be delivering this outside of their areas of expertise, lacking confidence and therefore commitment to the process.

There are several solutions to this; importantly, they all have a common theme. To distribute the load and focus on the areas where maximum student impact can be made with the least possible "effort".

Creating themed weeks or events is an excellent way to launch or highlight a specific part of a school's careers programme. It might be to tie in with a school theme or national initiative or simply be a way to kick off or round up the year. Whatever the reason, as an introduction, they are a great way for teachers to begin to find their way.

> Instead of taking over the timetabled lessons for this event, first look at what is already planned to be taught. There is no sense in stopping normal lessons, unless it is strictly necessary, in order to deliver this. It is time to work with staff to incorporate the theme into what they have already planned.
>
> - English lessons could theme creative writing around imagining a future where net zero is, or isn't, met. Or persuasive writing can be tailored to be letters addressed to the local MP or Councillors, convincing them to back local initiatives, possibly at the school itself.
> - Maths lessons might be themed around the calculations of saving money through the introduction of green technologies.
> - Science, well science lessons are pretty much tailored to this; there aren't many themes that can't cycle back to future sustainability.
> - PSH(C)E, depending on the topic and theme being followed, encourages students to understand their own relationship with the world around them and that their contributions to the future matter.
>
> These are just a few examples, across a handful of subjects around a single theme. The skill lies in the mastery of subject leaders and their ability to communicate with their class teachers the relevance of their subject to the world outside of the classroom. The work on the classroom floor is all about inspiration and creating a dynamic learning environment for students.

Developing the skill set to introduce these twists and tweaks to lesson theming is a core element of any integrated careers programme. As confidence in ability builds, so too does the capacity for teachers to build this process into their practice. It means that more themed events or periods can be built into the school calendar. Importantly, without the need for a centralised member of staff to plan the whole affair. All it takes is advanced warning and a centralised driver to support and guide and, importantly, not plan.

> **STAFF SUPPORT RESOURCE**
>
> Net zero, while this is significant from a national view, is not the only themed opportunity that is available throughout the year. Other event/themed weeks which could be easily adapted in this manner include:
>
> ### Science/STE(A)M Week
>
> Make use of whole school assemblies to bookend the week – start by introducing the theme students will be focusing on, and end by celebrating the successes of the week's work. You could also invite a special guest speaker to talk about their career in science and the significance it holds in their life and in society as a whole. Reaching out to local universities and sixth forms/colleges is a decent shout for this.
>
> Make it a standard across the school that all lessons should be themed or tilted towards STE(A)M. Art lessons can focus on colour theory, using natural beauty, such as flowers and galaxies, as stimuli. English and literacy lessons can focus on communicating scientific ideas or concepts previously learnt or picked up throughout the week. When it comes to independent or group reading, where possible, select texts which explore themes of science and science fiction and encourage students to see the differences in the themes.
>
> ### World Book Day
>
> This is a wonderful day and provides ample opportunity to support students in envisioning a vibrant future for themselves through the medium of role-play and literary engagement.
>
> In terms of bringing this into the fold of careers learning, there are several threads which can be pulled at. Ask students to research the career profile of the character they've dressed up as. Then, task them with creating a diary entry from that character's perspective, describing how they go about their job or day outside

of the story they inhabit. In addition to this, encourage staff who dress up to take on the persona of their chosen fictional or real-life characters. Interacting with students in character allows students to experience alternative points of view and engage in role-play with people in situations and professions they might not otherwise encounter.

Finally, remember that all books have authors. Their stories are never straightforward and simple. They are full of twists and turns which lead to their moments of inspiration that have created the characters which students and staff alike have come to adore. Share it.

Earth Day

Much like the theme of net zero, Earth Day and other such themed days are an excellent opportunity for students to engage with the world beyond the end of their noses. Using every opportunity in the school day to make students aware of and engage with this markedly increases its impact and messaging. The novelty of learning about traditionally scientific ideas within the framing of a music lesson or incorporated into their lunch menu, mirrors the wider situation at play. Turning the schools into a microcosm of the world outside of it. The world doesn't exist in nice segmented categories; everything is connected, and for this day, so too is the school.

Healthy Eating Week

Don't let this be the sole responsibility of the canteen to put on a healthy spread for students throughout the week. Give students the opportunity to explore the significance of maintaining a healthy lifestyle and which careers and jobs are related to this ever-growing industry.

While this might not be the most applicable to all subjects, it can certainly be incorporated into many. Science can look at how different jobs support people in promoting and maintaining healthy lifestyles; Art can explore how different foods are advertised to people and the jobs that do it. Ultimately it is about being creative and supporting teachers and staff to take a risk and make the links.

Black History Month

Black History Month is already a well-resourced and supported time of the school year with lots of resources for subjects to make use of to support its delivery and celebration. From a careers integration perspective, the additional impact and longevity of it comes from the cross-curricular commitment to it. While it can be simple to rely on History, PHS(C)E lessons and assemblies to do the heavy lifting, demonstrating to students its significance in all subjects across the board helps to deliver its message in a much more meaningful way.

History lessons can explore key figures and movements, such as the Civil Rights movement. Science has the opportunity to highlight contributions and discoveries made within various fields. English lessons could focus their guided reading, however, alongside this, providing students the opportunity to pause and reflect on the different perspectives and experiences within it can often be more poignant.

World Ocean Day

As with many days that are linked to the natural world and raising awareness, it can be very easy to let this sit solely within one or two lessons. But making it a whole-school event and using every opportunity to address it will raise its profile by orders of magnitude.

Using English lessons to engage students in exercising their writing techniques to produce imaginative and beautiful pieces of creative writing or storytelling based on the world's oceans. This would enable them to make use of the knowledge gained from science lessons, the trends of most polluted areas in geography and the journey that has led to our current situation in history.

Art Week

Incorporating Art into different lessons can be very straightforward, but can just as easily become very perfunctory and two-dimensional. It shouldn't be a case of completing artistic tasks under the guise of another lesson. Such as drawing a picture of what you think a character from a story might look like, or creating a model of a geographical feature, just for the sake of it. Activities like this can be completed in a normal lesson; it is not specific about Art Week.

This week can be an opportunity to demonstrate the artistic beauty and talent present in all subjects, and to draw them to the surface. The history books of biology are littered with beautiful renderings of specimens and samples. They were not drawn because the illustrator wanted to create art, but because they served a purpose. Using science lesson time to explore this and get students to create their own, that emphasises accuracy over composition, creates that tangible link between art and science which is so often overlooked. Similarly, geography and history lessons explore the history of cartography and the artistic licensing that took place with the very first maps to be drawn and published.

Enterprise Week

Enterprise weeks are fantastic opportunities for all students to experience the combined power that comes when all subjects focus on a single objective. Tasking them to work in groups on a project focused on an enterprising theme, which very well could be any of the before mentioned, allows them to peek behind the curtain and see where all of their learning is heading. Students of this age group have vivid and powerful imaginations which can be channelled and harnessed into creative projects like these.

Utilise the three "core" subjects to support and enhance the learning process. Science can provide a logical backbone and underpin the theory, English can develop creative and imaginative ways to present ideas, and Maths can be used to evidence and support decision-making and problem-solving along the way. Clearly there is more to the school day than these three subjects. However, they form a strong basis for everything else that follows; often it is the students who make some of the most interesting and profound links as they explore the process. Particularly when references are made back to learning earlier on in the day or week, seemingly out of nowhere.

Action checklist

- ☑ Choose an upcoming themed week or event in your school calendar (e.g. World Book Day, Science Week, Earth Day). Instead of planning a separate "careers activity", work with your subject team on how to weave career-related angles into your existing lesson plans for that week across different subjects.
  Think: careers integration, not careers isolation.

- ☑ Take one upcoming week's worth of lesson plans for your class. Quickly scan each lesson and jot down one potential "career connection" or skill link that already exists. It doesn't have to be a major overhaul, just highlight what's already there.
  Think: uncovering existing links, not reinventing the wheel.

- ☑ In one lesson this week, when you introduce a concept that might seem abstract or disconnected from "real life", pause and ask your students: "Where might someone use this skill/knowledge outside of school?" or "What kinds of jobs might involve this?" Be open to all answers and value their contributions.
  Think: making learning relevant, one "why" at a time.

4 | Curriculum review: Embedding careers

Summary points

Embedding Careers Learning into Teaching

Support all staff with the delivery of careers education, such that it is not the responsibility of a single person to ensure its delivery; it is a collective effort.

Auditing the Curriculum for Careers Learning

Using simple but effective techniques, such as subject-specific post-it note exercises, staff can take ownership of identifying and enhancing career connections within their subjects and classrooms.

Making Careers Education Accessible and Actionable

Supporting teachers to incorporate career education into their everyday practices to build ownership, relevance, and sustainability, ensuring students continuously see the value of their learning in the real world.

Loading the responsibility of planning and distribution of career-related learning within the curriculum, particularly during intense, themed weeks or events, on staff, is hugely labour-intensive. It runs the risk of failing to build a meaningful legacy. Particularly when it sits with a specific member of staff in addition to their daily role.

Relying on one person to plan and prepare all resources is not an effective use of time. Equally, no matter how excellent that teacher is, after a while it will become repetitive and formulaic. The staff delivering it will lack ownership, and students will start to see through the cracks. Spending time supporting all staff in the skill of integrating generalised careers learning into their practice will enable them to develop their own approach to lesson adaptation. More importantly, it will allow this approach to develop organically within their teaching.

To stress this point further, an organic approach to careers learning is an incredibly powerful tool. For staff, once they have initially been supported in finding their unique way of building it into their practice, it becomes second nature – just part of how they run their classroom. For students, this simply becomes part of their day, part of how they learn. They are incredibly resilient and adaptable and will quickly learn to expect this as part of their routine. Students are naturally curious; providing them with the "why" meaning to their learning instils them with an understanding of the purpose of their education. Powerful message, not to be underestimated.

Expanding the careers learning beyond stand-alone events/weeks can sound like a huge amount of work, going against one of the prime directives of this book. However, with a logical approach that builds itself into existing school life, it rapidly becomes a lot more achievable.

As with starting anything new, with staff just as much as with students, start small, start with quick wins, start with confidence building, and start with hearts as well as minds.

Learning point

Start with an existing curriculum; the format in which this will be found is going to be highly dependent on the setting, but, as will become apparent, this is largely irrelevant. An important aspect, however, is that it is a progressive scheme that builds year on year. Developed around the concept of accumulated experience and that sets a series of levelled learning objectives. Sometimes referred to as a spiralled curriculum. In all likelihood this will be a scheme of work with specific descriptors that identify the teaching and learning that needs to occur within each lesson. Now set this aside; it will be important, but not just yet.

On a nice large piece of paper, go A3; even better, push the boat out and go A2! For each, title it with their class year group. With the teaching cohort in front of you, ask them to populate it with what they do for one year in their classroom that they would consider careers education. Now, depending on how you phrase this and the support you offer, you will get an array of answers being generated, in terms of the quantity and specificity. The important thing is to put together a picture of the landscape from the classroom teacher's point of view at this particular moment in time. Starting to get them thinking about how they feel they contribute to the students' future preparedness. Now pop them to the side. You are going to be building up quite the sideboard here.

This might have seemed like a rather arbitrary task. However, it is an essential stage that will enable you to empower staff to be able to start to see careers learning as something deeper than a bolt onto the side of the curriculum. If they cannot see its purpose and where it fits in with what is already being done, then the level of resistance to its adoption will be significantly harder.

> At this point, it is time to introduce the importance of careers education at all stages of a student's school experience. Embedding a solid base into the primary curriculum is the starting point for all of this. A gentle reminder that this is not about telling students about jobs that exist, jobs they could have, or jobs that you have done. These all have their places, but they are not what careers education is. Careers education or future preparedness or careers learning are all about showing young people the importance of their education. It is about preparing them for an unknown world of work in the future. That their personal development and skills utilisation and articulation will be universal currency in this climate.

As a side note, this is a good time to introduce how careers education could work within your context. Hit home the point that this is an effort that must be committed to by everyone within a school and not just the few. Equally, there is no significant change about to occur in their daily practice or routine. It is all about highlighting what is already there and shining a light on what might have otherwise gone unnoticed.

> It wouldn't be staff training without them, so get out the post-it notes (other brightly coloured square sticky notes are available) and bring back those progressive curriculum plans. It is time for subject leaders to start looking at their curriculums with a new light and a new focus.
>
> They need to change hats, stop thinking like the class teacher of one year group and start thinking as the curriculum leader. Ask them to work through their curriculums and make a note on a post-it every time they identify an area where careers-related learning takes place, regardless of year group. They should note the concept which is being taught/learnt as well as the topic/lesson, reasons to become clear shortly.
>
> This can be from the overt, such as when identification or reference is made to particular careers or jobs, within topics or lessons. Or it can be more subtle (hint, these are the ones you want to encourage), such as opportunities for cross-curricular or contextual learning, interpersonal skill development or big picture thinking, to name just a few. At this stage it is often helpful to introduce a framework (addressed later on in this book) for staff to work from, so that they have a reference point.
>
> Now, for this next part, it is important that each identifiable point is on its own post-it and has the year group associated with it at the top. If the same point applies to two year groups, unfortunately, this will need to be written twice, sorry. Reiterate the need to be as comprehensive as possible.

At this point, things will start to get a bit messy and a bit chaotic. This is good; there will be lots of pieces of paper on tables, and no doubt a bit of confusion as to where all of this is headed. Stick with it, you're nearly there, it's time to start bringing it all together.

> A lovely little trick here is to give each subject their own colour; it will make the final step visually more interesting and impactful. All of the post-it notes now need to make their way onto the original A3 (or A2) piece of paper, one for each of the year groups. There doesn't need to be any pomp or ceremony for this, just get them stuck on.

What you will be left with is each year group/class having a myriad of coloured paper spread across it displaying all of the learning that is taking place within each year group that has the sole purpose of providing context and meaning to the curriculum. It will provide each classroom with a comprehensive list, produced by the staff that know the subjects best as well as the staff who know the students and age-specific development best, which encapsulates every aspect of a student's experience that year.

Whether this is digitised or converted into a logical format is a decision best left with you, the person reading/using this. How it will be implemented by staff in the long- and short-term planning of lessons is also yours. Regardless of the format, it needs to have the following qualities:

- Usability
  - The ability to be picked up by a newly qualified teacher, teaching assistant, or experienced teacher and understand the relevance and application to their practice.
  - There shouldn't be a need to spend hours decoding multiple documents and reference documents. It should be "pick up and go".
- Logic
  - Clearly identifiable in its links to the structure of the curriculum along with any skills progression documents and resources.
  - Linked or referenced within the wider school's ethos, it should be seamless in its logic in its application to daily school life.
- Simplicity
  - There is nothing worse than annotations that only make sense to the one who created them. Make sure all the points are straightforward and easily understood.
    - "Bricklayers need to use measurements" = bad.
    - "Ref: Bricklaying – no. of bricks needed to build wall, needs to know length for bricks in row, need to know height for no. of rows" = better.

- o "Ref: Bricklaying – demo no. of bricks needed to make a wall, important link to real-world maths, ext. independent work out no. bricks needed for wall" = best.
- Always put yourself in the position of a teacher who is turning up for their first day and seeing this document for the first time out of context. Would they understand its purpose and application?

STAFF SUPPORT RESOURCE

Examples and styles of curriculum audits.

Auditing is all about preparation and making it abundantly clear what needs to be done. There are several different approaches available depending on resources, method of delivery and staff dynamics. What works best for you is dependant on many factors, one of which is to make sure that you have a chosen framework that suits your school and serves the needs of the students. More can be found on this in Part III – *Putting frameworks into action*.

Simple job vs skills audit

This process is a quick and dirty system that allows for a fast snapshot of a curriculum that can be completed with or without training in advance. It requires staff to think about their curriculums through two lenses: job awareness and skill development, two core strands of any careers programme.

Careers framework excerpt

Category	Subcategory	Key stage	Coding
Reference to "job"	Healthcare: e.g. *Doctor, Nurse, Paramedic*	1	1J.He
Reference to "job"	Healthcare: e.g. *Pharmacist, Physiotherapist, Optician*	2	2J.He
Reference to "job"	Construction: e.g. *Builder, Plumber, Electrician*	1	1J.Co
Reference to "job"	Construction: e.g. *Architect. Civil Engineer, Surveyor*	2	2J.Co
...	...	...	...

Embedding Careers in the Curriculum

Category	Subcategory	Key stage	Coding
Reference to "skill"	Communication: taking turns speaking, listening to others, asking questions, and explaining thoughts.	1	1S.C
Reference to "skill"	Communication: working in teams, sharing ideas, asking questions, listening carefully, and presenting information clearly.	2	2S.C
Reference to "skill"	Problem-Solving: exploring ideas, trying different solutions, asking for help, and learning through play.	1	1S.P
Reference to "skill"	Problem-Solving: working in teams, brainstorming ideas, testing solutions, and learning from mistakes.	2	2S.P
...	...	...	...

This table can be extended as far as required in terms of job/industry sectors and skills.

Geography (human and physical) skills progression excerpt:

KS1	KS2 (lower)	KS2 (higher)
Learn about the seasons. Identify the four seasons and their changes. Use basic geographical vocabulary in reference to the seasons and weather. **1S.C**	Learn what a climate zone is and identify them on a world map. **2S.P** Understand and describe the difference between human and physical geography. Learn about the different biomes of the world and locate them on a world map.	Explain how physical features form, why they are significant and how they change over time. **2S.C** Learn about dams and describe their different uses, such as flood prevention and power. **2J.Co** Explore human geography and human impact on our environment.

This has created a reference document for any new or absent, members of staff to pick up when they are planning their lessons to see where different progression points can be used to highlight particular elements of the careers programme. It is not about every lesson, every day, every year delivering every point. It is holistic. Over the course of their school life they will be exposed to everything at times and in places where it is most pertinent and relevant.

The "what?" and the "where?"

This is all about asking staff to inhabit their subject and think big. This is more time intensive and will almost certainly require support for staff to enable them to begin to think about their subject as more than a series of learning objectives. It has the advantage of its final results providing all the information required to create posters or subject resources which can be displayed and shared to celebrate what the subject is worth beyond the factual learning.

The gist of it is very straightforward: for each of the specification points of your chosen framework, identify what your subject does to address it and where can it be found. Simple, right? The knack to making this of worth is to ensure that the statements are as specific as possible. To take history as an example, to say that history addresses the concept of "discovering different jobs and what they involve" by talking about jobs from the past, or within each topic, is obvious. This is a very generic statement and could apply to any lesson, in any school, in any part of the country. Make the answers specific to your school and your curriculum.

Subject: History   **Theme:** Career readiness

Subpoints	KS1 – What?	KS1 – Where?
The World of Work *Discover different jobs people do and what they involve*	Study of Victorian Britain explores the range of jobs people held, with a focus on the roles that people had in society. We pose the questions: Why does this job still exist 100 years later? What is the modern equivalent of this job?	Year 2 – The Victorians – introduction to Victorian society
Employability Skills *Learn how to work with others*	Why do we call inventors, inventors? Why do we still talk about these people today? We examine the importance of free thinkers and the importance of social justice with key figures of the past.	Year 1 – Influential people from the past – Edison and the light bulb

Embedding Careers in the Curriculum

Subpoints	KS2 – What?	KS2 – Where?
The World of Work *Start to understand how work helps people and society and learn about different industries*	Students develop an understanding of the significance of technological revolutions, such as the stone age and compare this to modern changes in technological advancements such as AI.	Year 3 – Stone Age Britain – The first revolution
Employability Skills *Work in teams, share ideas, and communicate clearly*	Students understand the importance of democracy and why it has been a pillar of society for the past 200 years.	Year 5 – the Ancient Greeks – The big ideas

There is the option, too, to add an additional layer highlighting jobs and industry to all of the topics that are being covered, this is especially effective in subjects that can appear to students, repetitive, such as maths, English, or music.

Linked industry

Linking local, national, and international companies, employment sectors and job roles* to the specific moments of learning in the classroom. The essence of it is to first get staff to think about the legacy of their subject in students' lives and then to specifically make links to their lesson planning and delivery. There is the option to keep it simple with direct reference or option to develop it further with inclusion of industry/job descriptions, related information or even links to specific learning objectives.

These are very loose and interchangeable terms, it's really about highlighting the links between the curriculum and the world of work beyond the classroom.

Subject: Maths

Topic: Money	Linked Industry	Linked Companies	Linked Jobs
Coin Value	- Finance - Banking - Self-employed - Construction - Charities - Hospitality	- Barclays Bank - Kier Construction - Cancer Research	- Self-employed - Project Manager - Fundraising - Restaurant Manager - Chef

Topic: Money	Linked Industry	Linked Companies	Linked Jobs
Measurement	- Horticulture - Aviation - Mechanics - Sport - Construction	- Quickfit - British Airways - Mace - Chelsea FC	- Landscape Gardener - Motor Mechanic - Surveyor - Sports Coach - Carpenter - Pilot

This audit model should not be used alone; there is a real risk that teachers could rely on this solely for their careers input to teaching which would be incredibly limiting. While it does promote the ethos of "you can't be what you can't see", it does not contribute to the wider development of a student's education to prepare them for the next steps. Use with caution.

Action checklist

☑ Dedicate a department meeting (or a focused team session) to curriculum auditing. Use a simple method like the "post-it note" exercise. Ask teachers to review one unit of their curriculum and identify existing career links and skills development opportunities.
Think: collective curriculum ownership.

☑ Choose one subject area and conduct a simplified "Job vs Skills" audit. Use the provided framework example as a starting point. Focus on identifying explicit job references and implicit skill development within that subject's curriculum.
Think: targeted audit for quick wins.

☑ If you have a careers curriculum map, conduct a "usability test". Ask an early career teacher (ECT), teaching assistant (TA), or a teacher unfamiliar with careers initiatives to review the map. Can they easily understand its relevance and application to their practice? Identify areas for simplification and clarity.
Think: "pick up and go" curriculum design.

5 | Finding the "why": Connecting learning to careers

Summary points

Giving Meaning to the "Meaningless"
Lessons that can seem irrelevant to students can be made engaging by framing them within real-world contexts, helping students see their value beyond the classroom.

Encouraging Dynamic Questioning for Real-World Connections
Strategic questioning can link lessons to future career pathways, sparking critical thinking, and showing students the practical application of their learning.

The Challenge of Integrating Careers Learning into Every Lesson
Embedding careers education into each lesson sounds great but can overwhelm teachers. A more manageable approach is needed to make it relevant without extra planning.

Knowing that careers learning has the potential to be anywhere at any time, unlocks a smorgasbord of possibilities which can be used to maximum effect. Planning careers into every single lesson, every single day however is a nightmare. It is beyond time-consuming; it is all-encompassing. For some this might be exciting, but for the majority this is deal-breaking and highly likely to end in tears, or at the very least, tantrums.

It is important, then, that a solution is found that will enable every learning opportunity to become a relevant careers learning opportunity. Without the onus being placed on staff to plan it into everything. A Holy Grail you say?

While a Holy Grail may be too good to be true, a close second is to be able to provide teachers with a crib sheet. One which can be used within their classrooms for an array of subjects without the need for specific careers-y expertise. And it all lies in the questioning. Knowing that you have an arsenal of strategies up your sleeve can be incredibly valuable. These can be called upon not only to enrich a student's learning or understanding, but also to serve as impromptu extension tasks for those who complete work at rocket speed.

> **Learning point**
>
> A computing topic in Year 4 is currently focusing on security and privacy on the internet. Students are learning about how to protect themselves online from identity fraud and theft and how to ensure their personal data is secure. This is a fairly factual concept with the gist of it essentially being: here is a series of things you need to do and here is why you need to do it. No matter how much passion is injected into it, let's face it, at the end of the day it's pretty dry.

This is a common theme which teachers are often faced with. Here is a fact which must be taught and learnt, there is very little opportunity for self-discovery for the student to arrive at this from an organic process. Or, for that matter, for them to have an appreciation for the deeper concept and intricacies will simply require a higher level of education. So what now, teach it as a fact and move on? Or see where the learning takes them. Time to be a little more dynamic and get them to think about it in a slightly different way that applies their learning in a different context.

> Asking the simple question of "what information is unique to you?" might seem very simple and straightforward. But it has the potential to open a dialogue that goes beyond the scope of the curriculum, raising some very important issues that students need to be aware of. Certainly, there are people far more qualified to discuss and interrogate this further. The simple act of showing students "why" they are learning a fact is so important if the value of that fact is to be realised. Otherwise, it will remain just that, a fact, a stand-alone statement that may well be true, but doesn't necessarily bear meaning to the one who learnt it.

There will always be students who struggle to engage with or grasp the conceptual nature of many lessons that are being taught. Finding the "in" is key; careers-related learning is often the last turned to, but often the most effective.

5| Finding the "Why": Connecting Learning to Careers

> **Author's note**
>
> To raise a tangential point here, this is true of all subjects and lessons; every student is an individual. Their uniqueness means that they will find engagement in some subjects easier than others. While this example is specific to computing, its theory is universal and applicable to all subjects and all students; it is about finding the right question for the right moment.

> This lesson's strength lies in its interconnectedness, naturally weaving in aspects of the wider curriculum, such as PSH(C)E, which often stands alone. This cross-pollination of subjects isn't just good pedagogy; it mirrors the reality students will encounter beyond education. The more they grasp that knowledge isn't siloed, that skills and understanding from different areas intertwine, the better prepared they'll be for the complexities of the modern world and their future careers. Collaboration across disciplines, drawing on diverse skill sets, and understanding the broader context of any task are increasingly vital in professional life. Recognising this interconnectedness now helps foster adaptability, a crucial life skill for navigating an ever-evolving job market.

Students are often the best instigators of these moments; they will ask one question back at you, often to the internal horror of the teacher: "why?" But what a perfect moment to show that there is a wider learning at stake that is not just relevant to school, but also to the larger issue at hand, life. Being ready with a couple of stock responses is good. Even better is to have it preempted and incorporate it into the lesson is better. With a few strategic questions in the back pocket, the students will answer their own questions before they even ask them.

> Therefore, to continue the narrative of this learning point, we must acknowledge that not all students will readily engage with every subject or lesson. Sometimes this can be anticipated; it will often be built into the lesson plan, or the teaching staff have enough of a relationship to accommodate in advance. Then there will be the moments when it is not foreseen and in order to maintain lesson momentum; it is important to be able to, off the cuff, give students insight into the purpose of their learning. Crucially, this mirrors the need in professional life to understand the "why" behind tasks. Avoiding dismissive phrases like "you just need to know it" is vital, as it undermines the development of critical thinking and the ability to connect learning to purpose – a key skill for career progression and personal motivation.

> Swinging back to the start, using the question, as before "what makes you unique?" and then "Why would someone want to know this? What could they do with this information?" effectively primes students to consider the value and application of their learning. This fosters a mindset of inquiry and self-discovery, essential for lifelong learning and career development. By encouraging students to articulate the relevance themselves, they develop crucial skills in understanding the "so what?" – a vital aspect of professional communication and problem-solving. This self-directed understanding, where students essentially teach themselves, builds confidence and initiative, qualities highly sought after in the workplace.

When working with staff, remember to remind them that this is not a miracle fix, it will take time, practice, and learning from mistakes. The skill of being able to guide learning purely through conversation and inspire students to think differently, is hard, don't give up on it.

Do not underestimate the power of having an arsenal of questions, or at the least a template of question types and styles that can be applied to any given situation when their need becomes apparent. This will have a far wider-reaching impact than just the scenario stated above. A confident teacher will be able to provide context and motivation to students to engage them in the lesson, which might otherwise be inaccessible to them.

As with all things in the classroom, consistency is key. It will take time to embed new practices, but considerably longer to practise it and become confident to a point where it is second nature. This is not a quick fix; give it time.

IN-CLASS RESOURCE

Questioning styles that can be used within the classroom or wider school setting seek to develop student learning and cognition while also promoting a forward-thinking and a future-ready mentality in students.

Below is a summary of typical questioning styles that can be used in most lessons, regardless of subject or content. Often referred to as "dynamic" questioning or "extension" questions. Regardless of the name they are given, they are generally universal, they just need to have the theme/content of them changed to fit in with the teaching or conversation that is being had.

No wrong answer

Questions of this type promote "outside the box" thinking in students. They make for excellent extension questions for students who typically finish their work quickly or as introductory questions to stimulate thinking before topics or concepts have been delivered. Examples include:

- What connects the seasons on Earth and the Football Association (FA) Cup?
- Who would be a better teacher: *some random YouTuber* or Henry VIII? Convince me.
- How long a line can you draw with a single pencil? Show your workings.

What if?

Some of the greatest moments in a classroom come from these questions. There is simply no better way to derail a physics teacher than to ask them, "what if...?" Why? Because they form the heart of learning, every human development, and have underpinned every invention of the past 12,000 years. It optimises the curiosity that is at the heart of the human condition. Instil this love into your students' lives and learning and you have done your job. Examples include:

- What if we didn't have seasons? How would our country look different?
- What if you could speak directly to a Victorian child? What would you tell them? How would this change their lives?
- What would happen if, overnight, everyone started to speak French, what would you do?

Why?

Asking students why is the simplest question you can ask; however, it can be easily misused and wasted opportunities which lose their potency. They generally fall into two categories: to encourage students to justify their own reasoning or to think deeper on the application of a concept within a lesson. Examples include:

- Why have you decided upon this answer/conclusion? Justify your opinion
- Why did the character react/act in that way? What other ways could they have acted? How would this have impacted the rest of the story?
- Why do you think a plant grows better in sunlight than under a light bulb?

Bridging the gap

Bridging the gap questions are all about making the links between different areas of student experience. They might be to bring together two subjects to demonstrate the universality of a concept. It could be used to test students' interdisciplinary knowledge and their ability to make connections through logical reasoning. It can be used to provide an "in" for students who struggle to find motivation for subjects or topics they find uninteresting. Examples include:

- When do you need to be able to use maths in a PE lesson?
- How many examples can you come up with that link science and art? Bonus points for anyone that can come up with more than five.
- How can understanding and using English be useful in a geography lesson?

Find me a job

Questions of this nature should be used sparingly, but they are often the go-to questions for teachers who are bringing careers into the classroom. They run the risk of polarising groups of students if it is misjudged. The premise is very simple, asking the student to find examples of which jobs require the current skill or knowledge and how they might use them. It should be emphasised that obvious answers simply will not do, just because you are studying football in PE does not mean that everyone will be a footballer. Examples include:

- Which jobs do you think will need you to know about the content of today's lesson?
- How many different jobs do you think today's lesson applies to? How do those jobs use these ideas?
- Find me a job that doesn't use maths/English/science/PE. Prove it.

Break it down

A slightly more nuanced line of questioning for students to pick up on; they will likely need coaching in order to be able to gain the most from it. At its heart, it is all about supporting students to be able to break down their learning into its fundamental parts. A misconception is that these types of questions are best used as extensions for high-ability students. With a little support and nudging, these make excellent questions to engage any learner.

5| Finding the "Why": Connecting Learning to Careers

- What is more important for understanding and learning in today's lesson: teamwork, problem-solving, or positivity? Why have you chosen that one over the other two?
- What are the key steps to carrying out an investigation in science? What would be the consequence of removing the prediction step? Why is this a crucial part of a meaningful investigation?
- Why did the story start at the point it did? Why didn't we start it at the point where it got exciting?

STAFF SUPPORT RESOURCE

How to frame and teach those elements of the curriculum that are just dry.

Giving meaning to the "meaningless". Potentially a cruel statement, but a little more understandable from a student's perspective. There are lessons or concepts which can seem meaningless or arbitrary to students, especially when compared to modern life. While, depending on your opinion on the matter, this may very well be true, they are still vital in a student's education. In some cases, there is no getting away from it; it's part of the national curriculum. Providing wider context and reasoning behind particular elements will not only greatly support student engagement; but also develop more than just the obvious objective outcomes. Framing is everything.

Spelling tests

Perception: Unnecessary in the modern age with the use of spellcheck and intelligent AI models, there is no need for the ability to memorise spellings of words. What is the point in learning by rote? It's an old-fashioned way of learning that is not reflective of the modern world, it causes undue stress on students and parents. Rewarding only those who have better memory than others and putting SEND students at a marked disadvantage against their peers.

Solution: Increased skill in spelling correctly and understanding the nature of orthography is worth much more to young people than simply needing to use spellcheck less often. As students learn spelling rules and language trends, they develop a deeper grasp of how language works. Gradually, this process helps them find their own voice and discover the unique patterns of language that belong to them. It is all well and good to make use of AI to generate content and prose; but its overuse in this field can serve to lose the patter of the author. This isn't always the easiest message to get through to students, it has to be demonstrated. Setting the spellings into context of wider activities and including other measures of success that enable all students to find a level of gratisfaction from it helps. For example: creative uses of spelling within sentences, correct and creative uses of grammar and sentence structure, or correct use of capital letters and punctuation. All of these promote the deeper learning of a spelling test, while creating success criteria that are a lot more accessible and inclusive to the students. Ultimately, strong spelling skills contribute significantly to professional credibility and effective written communication, both of which are crucial for career success. While spellcheckers are useful tools, the underlying ability to spell accurately demonstrates attention to detail and linguistic competence, qualities valued across various professions. Furthermore, a strong grasp of language, fostered through learning orthography, enhances overall literacy, a fundamental life skill impacting everything from understanding contracts to writing clear and concise communications.

Mental arithmetic/times tables

Perception: Memorising and recalling times tables by rote is outdated. We have been using calculators for longer than most of the students' parents have been alive. Access to technology is almost instantaneous, so why would we need to memorise something which can be done for us, and often faster. With simple automation almost taken for granted nowadays, this, much like many pure memory recall activities, can seem arbitrary.

Solution: The destination of learning is so often mistaken for the point of learning. In reality, the journey holds far greater significance for a student's long-term success and is even more relevant to their future professional lives. Mental arithmetic and the learning of times tables is a prime example, what was once essential before the rise of accessible technology is now largely redundant. However, its secondary learning, now its primary, is where the emphasis should be placed, if it is going to continue to be taught. Placing the focus on, and further rewarding, the process is the way to bring this into the modern day. Showing students the importance of dedicated and routine repetition is a fundamental element of learning. Developing self-disciplined techniques to support this requires a regimented, systematic approach, well, here it is. The true value lies not in the outdated necessity of recall but in the cultivation of fundamental learning skills. By shifting our focus to the *process*, we highlight the development of systematic repetition, pattern recognition, memory strategies, and concentration. Rewarding effort, progress, and the application of varied learning techniques underscores that the journey itself builds crucial self-discipline and learning methodologies applicable far beyond multiplication tables.

Homework

Perception: We work hard enough at school; why should we do more work at home? An ever increasingly common opinion is that the home should be for things students want to do and not be used to complete more school work, which should've been completed in school.

Solution: Homework that is set must, above all else, be meaningful. Otherwise don't set it. There must be a clear reason and meaning for it and not a continuation of the work that was completed in the classroom. Homework is a prime opportunity to set extended project work that provides a framework for students to apply the learning in a different environment. When set right, pitched in such a way that they can explore their creativity and pursue curiosity and interests it can help put learning into context and broaden the horizons of possibility. It is the primary vessel for bridging the gap between learning in the classroom and independently taking learning outside. Instilling a mindset of application and exploration. Crucially, this mirrors the demands of many future careers where independent work, project management, and self-directed learning are paramount. Meaningful homework fosters the very life skills needed to thrive professionally: initiative, time management, and the ability to see a task through to completion without constant supervision.

Sitting SATS/standardised assessments

Perception: As with many terminal exams, there are few points in non-educational life where you will need to recall reams of facts or complete tasks in isolation without some form of external support. Granted, in the distant past when formal education was becoming widely established, there was a genuine need for the art of memorising, recalling, and applying vast amounts of information. There were also clear benefits gained from mastering these skills at the time. But, and this is quite a significant "but", we are living in the world of today, not yesterday, this is much less relevant. Modern life, with all of its advancements, does not have the same requirements. Recall is often more available and more reliable when technology, such as the internet, is used correctly. So why sit a test which is only testing how well I can remember something that I'm probably not even that interested in or will ever need to remember again?

Solution: Exams need a bit of a PR boost, a shift of perspective. Of course, their purpose for teachers and schools has not widely changed; their purpose for students, however, has. Emphasising that while they are used to assess acquired knowledge, the benefit they provide students is a little more subtle. Tests allow students to test their performance under pressure, often in lower stake scenarios than would afford them in their lives outside of school. Understanding that stress and anxiety are normal emotions that can be overcome to serve, rather than restrict. But the only way to do this is to be put into situations where this is triggered. Scary? Yes. Necessary? Yes. Little and often testing at low stakes, which rewards effort over accuracy, supports students to build up mental resilience and are better prepared to master their emotions when faced with testing situations. Safe failure is so much more valuable than all-or-nothing success. This ability to perform under pressure, to manage anxiety, and to build resilience through testing experiences are vital life skills, directly applicable to job interviews, presentations, and high-stakes situations encountered in many careers. Standardised assessments, therefore, offer a valuable training ground for developing emotional intelligence and coping mechanisms essential for career readiness.

Grammar and sentence structuring

Perception: There are a myriad of structural rules which need to be learnt over the course of school. How many of them will be used in our lives? How often will we actually need to write essays of text with all of the rules of language perfectly applied? There are so many programmes and apps out there which can restructure your work and suggest edits, why do they need to be memorised? There are better uses of time and effort than learning something that'll never be used.

Solution: Understanding grammar rules and being able to structure coherent and logical sentences helps students develop and uncover their unique voice. Over-reliance on technology to check and correct their work from basic inputs will only serve to dilute this. It brings them into the middle of the generic linguistic road. Demonstrating the impact a well-formed sentence can have on the reader and the emotions and feelings it draws to the surface is a good starting point. It may be necessary to make it more relatable, using the language of their role models and deciphering what makes their voices unique and powerful. Make use of inspirational speeches from celebrities or characters from films and break them down to look at their use of language and how they use grammatical structures to deliver their messages. It is all about showing students that grammar and sentence structuring is so much more important than writing words on a page. Oddly enough, it can be the make or break of the dream job of their futures. Effective communication, built upon a solid understanding of grammar and sentence structure, is a cornerstone of career readiness. Whether writing emails, presenting ideas, or collaborating with colleagues, the ability to articulate oneself clearly and persuasively is highly valued. Strong language skills foster confidence and professionalism, directly impacting future career success and overall life skills.

Action checklist

- [✓] Choose one lesson in your upcoming plans that students might perceive as "meaningless" or irrelevant to their lives (think spelling tests, times tables, grammar drills etc.). Identify at least two different ways you can reframe this lesson to highlight its real-world relevance and connect it to valuable skills beyond just the subject content.
  Think: finding the hidden value.

- [✓] Before an upcoming lesson, prepare at least three "dynamic questioning" prompts from the examples provided in the chapter. Intentionally weave these questions into your lesson delivery to encourage deeper thinking and real-world connections; don't just save them for extension activities.
  Think: questioning for connection and purpose.

- [✓] After a lesson where you've used dynamic questioning and reframed "meaningless" content, take a few minutes for a quick check-in with your students. Ask them, verbally or through a quick exit ticket: "Did today's lesson change your mind about when you might use this learning outside of school?" or "Did any questions today make you think differently about [topic]?"
  Think: student voice as your feedback loop.

6 | Preparing for the next step: Transition to secondary

Summary points

Strengthen Primary-Secondary School Connections
Use the final half-term of Year 6 to build deeper ties between primary and secondary schools through teacher visits, subject-based workshops, and interactive sessions, easing student transitions.

Reduce Transition Anxiety with Familiarity
Increase student exposure to secondary school teachers and teaching styles in a familiar primary setting, helping to normalise the change and alleviate fears about new environments.

Encourage Collaboration between Schools
Foster long-term partnerships between schools by creating shared projects, mentorship programmes, and joint initiatives that benefit both students and teachers, promoting a more interconnected education system.

The end of primary school is, for many students, the first moment they will recall moving through a significant transition in their education. It is a period of time that brings out a very mixed bag of emotion for them, as well as their parents. This is relatively well managed by schools; it has been going on a while now.

The structure of the Year 6 academic year is pretty rigid. For the vast majority of schools SATs examinations are an immovable pillar that marks the end of their time in primary education. The only thing is, it isn't, there is still a solid half-term, 150 hours, give or take, of lessons left for them to work through. Yes, there is an end-of-year show to prepare for and rounding off their time with the school. But this is a prime opportunity to look at the transition programme and give it the obligatory careers treatment.

> **Learning point**
>
> The standard routine for the final half-term is down to the individual schools. There are a couple of universal outcomes and revelations that come from it.
>
> - Students will make a visit to a taster day at their designated secondary school.
> - Students will deliver a show to the school and parents with the sole purpose of making as many adults in the room as possible cry.
> - There will be the core group who get a "bit too big for their boots". The big fish in a small pond lot.
> - The noticeable increase in cases of transition-derived anxiety among students.
>
> The degree to which these will manifest themselves is down to the individuals, but generally speaking, the final stretch will bring these out. So much so that the curriculum is written around it. In efforts to reduce the impact of this limbo time, there will be a marked increase in the number of school trips that take place or special events. As well as "transition" lessons where students are verbally prepared for the forthcoming changes.

Quite often, what happens is that this increase in non-standard activities further highlights the fact that this phase of their journey is coming to an end. In some cases actually increasing some of the issues they are seeking to avoid. Completely understandable from a student's perspective. This is a marked end to one phase of their education juxtaposed by a jarring start to the next. Going from the eldest in a small environment to the youngest in a much larger one.

> It can become a self-fulfilling prophecy that, over time, it becomes an ingrained part of school culture. These inevitabilities will always come to pass. With every year that arrives and moves on, it just becomes an accepted practice, to the point where it becomes expected practice. Students in younger years see it ahead of them and patiently await its inevitable arrival for when they find themselves in the same situation. It is therefore not just tolerated but embraced as a time of celebration and a chance to champion the journey students have taken during their time at the school. This period allows for activities that might otherwise be difficult to fit into a busy curriculum, such as school trips. It also provides time to prepare for the end-of-year farewell assembly and to create meaningful mementos for students as they move on.

6| Preparing for the Next Step: Transition to Secondary

To say that this is a missed opportunity might be a little extreme; the work that is being completed and the development that is taking place are invaluable and not to be lost. Having just said that, it is a wonderful coincidence that secondary schools find themselves with 20% less students that require teaching at the same point. So, at a time when students find themselves at the end of one school year with time to spare, the schools they will be shortly joining also find themselves with a decrease in the number of students in attendance. This is the moment to strengthen the ties between the primary schools and their local secondaries.

It is well known that preparation and exposure help to soften the blow of a large and significant change. The final half-term is the perfect time to reach out and take advantage of this fact.

> Yes, there will be the standard visits that are made from the local secondary schools to meet the students who will be joining them in September. They will introduce themselves and collect the details of those who will need additional support. You never know, they might even take the time to speak more openly with all of the students who are enrolled with them. At some point, they will also invite all of the students who are joining in September for a taster day to experience the secondary school environment. But all of this is necessary and the absolute minimum one would expect; there is so much more potential going to waste.
>
> Invite teachers from secondary schools to come and work with students (regardless of where they are actually leaving to in September), particularly around how lessons are taught and why they are the way they are. These are one of those rare opportunities in education where the concept of learning for the love of it is the only, obvious purpose. Bring in the local Head of Science to show students the wonders of the natural world and explain the true meaning of the scientific method and its application to so much more than science. Ask the Business Studies department to come and support an enterprise project by acting as mentors to the teams and becoming guest judges.
>
> It doesn't actually matter, really, what the subject being offered is. What's important is that they understand why they are there: they genuinely want to be there. They should be passionate about their subject, with the kind of love for it that only a proud parent can have.

The possible opportunities to take advantage of are kind of endless; it all comes down to the level of engagement you can leverage from the teachers. Relationships are everything. The initial impetus, though, is often best initiated through the leadership of each school and using their influence to drive those first engagements. Encouraging repeat engagement and asking schools to release and cover staff from their working days is not always the easiest. The benefits however, are numerous, with all parties gaining outcomes which they can find value in. Once that ball is rolling it just keeps going.

As with all things in education, legacy is key. Form relationships that go beyond individual teachers and bring schools together for long-term engagements. It will no longer be a chore, or calling in a favour; it will be just how it is.

Knowing the potential benefits that each party can gain from developing these relationships, engaging in a regular programme like this can go an awful long way to get the process moving.

The students

The students gain exposure to the next stage of their education, regardless of whether the teacher is coming from their intended secondary school or not. Unlike the taster day experiences, during these events, they are met in the middle. It is secondary content and themes being delivered in a safe place they know well. Some of the anxiety around the transition comes from the uncertainty. Uncertainty of a new environment and the unknown quantities around other students and, in particular, unknown teachers. This serves to reduce that factor, head-on.

The more interactions and touch points before the big move, the more the change becomes a natural one. Ultimately though, it highlights to students the interconnectivity of the world around them. They might think they exist in their own little bubbles, but there is a whole world out there waiting for them to join it. It's never the intended lesson in interactions such as these, but it is often the most important one; education does not stop when you leave the classroom.

The schools relationships and partnerships

Relationships are everything. With education increasingly becoming more and more siloed, building and maintaining connections with neighbouring schools is essential for long-term stability. As with the world outside of them, schools need to embrace a symbiotic relationship and interconnectivity with those around. The trading of favours is worth more than the exchange of money. Keeping students at the centre of every transaction and ensuring that everything is done with their long-term benefit in mind is crucial.

Partnership projects such as these are far more likely to gain traction and draw interest from other external parties. While this is never its motivating factor, it is something that can, and should be, monopolised upon. Where appropriate, it can be used to raise awareness of the work that is being done and promote the schools offer of above and beyond. Even encourage local businesses to join in on the action and really sell the interconnected message to students and school community as a whole.

The secondary school teachers

Building a profile with students before they join your classes in September goes a long way to securing meaningful relationships from the outset. The students you took the time to engage with on their turf, where they feel comfortable, will be far more willing to go the extra mile and respect your approach when you eventually teach them. Building that early connection makes a lasting difference. It also helps prepare students for the expectations of a secondary school lesson, which can often feel quite different and even jarring to fresh-faced Year 7s.

Again, it comes down to relationships. Taking this extra time to meet new students at their level and provide a point of familiarity come September pays off long term. They will be less likely to have behavioural issues. They will have a reputation as someone who can be more approachable and relatable to students, and they will have a bank of "goodwill" from the outset.

STAFF SUPPORT RESOURCE

How to get the most out of interschool partnerships.

Using recently departed Year 11 students

Not as morbid as it sounds. Offer additional work experience to Year 11 students who are on the "longest summer holidays of their lives". Inviting them to come in to work with some of the more vulnerable or trickier characters in their final weeks with you can help smooth their transition. This is a prime opportunity to use students who are already predisposed to wanting to work with young people. Use their recent experience of education to provide mentorship to the students who will benefit most from it.

The success of projects such as this lies in establishing a sustainable partnership between the primary and secondary schools. By making this a recurring annual opportunity, a tradition of peer mentorship can develop. Former primary students, now in Year 11, could return to inspire younger pupils, some of whom may have previously benefited from this very programme. This provides a sense of community, aspirational role models, and reinforces the value of giving back.

To initiate this, primary school staff could proactively reach out to their local secondary school(s) around the time Year 11 students finish their exams. This outreach could involve proposing a structured "summer mentorship programme" where interested Year 11 leavers are invited to volunteer for a set period. Teachers could then work with the secondary school to identify suitable students and coordinate their involvement in classrooms or with specific younger pupils. Building this communication channel into an annual routine would then establish the aforementioned long-term partnership.

Summer projects

Establishing a partnership with a local secondary school in order to set summer projects that will give students a focal point to take away over the summer break. This can be something as simple as a research task for a particular subject which will feed into their first topic upon arriving in September. Leading through to more complex activities which can set them up for joining extracurricular clubs, such as debate or science club.

It is important to note that this must not be a compulsory task. Nor should it be overly rewarded upon their arrival in September to prevent alienation and create an artificial divide among students from multiple schools. Equally, there is the counter-intuitive need to make sure that the students leaving your setting are not looked upon as favourable by taking part in these. This runs the risk of becoming detrimental if overdone; subtly is everything.

Early intervention mentorships

It isn't just the Year 11 students who have availability in the summer term. Many secondary schools will use this time for their Year 10 work experience programmes. Feeder primary schools are by far the most popular placement among them. Make use of their time with you; they don't just need to be teaching assistants for the duration of their time with you. By getting them to speak with Year 6 students about the upcoming transition process and their experiences of secondary school. This provides a chance to smooth out the transition by building links before the move even occurs. For your students they will have an automatic point of contact come September, creating a seed of familiarity upon arrival. They will also be in the perfect position to be able to highlight some of the tips and tricks to get a stronger start to the next phase of their lives.

Action checklist

- [✓] In the final half-term of Year 6, reach out to your local secondary school(s) and invite a subject specialist teacher (e.g. Head of Science, Maths, Art) to visit your primary school and deliver a taster session to Year 6. Focus on a subject that can spark curiosity and demonstrate the "love of learning" beyond just curriculum content.
Think: secondary expertise, primary setting.

- [✓] Collaborate with your linked secondary school to arrange a visit from their Year 7 (ideally alumni of your primary school, if possible). Have these Year 7 students come back to your primary to run an informal Q&A session with Year 6 students about their experiences of secondary school, focusing on demystifying the transition and building familiarity.
Think: peer-to-peer reassurance, relatable voices.

- [✓] Contact your local secondary school(s) to explore the possibility of a joint "summer project" for Year 6 students transitioning to Year 7. This could be a non-compulsory but fun project (e.g. a creative writing challenge, a local history investigation, a STEM design task) that students can work on during the summer holidays and potentially share with both primary and secondary staff in September.
Think: bridging the summer gap, building shared legacy.

PART II
Secondary

> We can grow up. We can leave the nest. We can fulfil the Destiny, make homes for ourselves among the stars, and become some combination of what we want to become and whatever our new environments challenge us to become.
>
> Octavia E. Butler, *Parable of the Talents*

Careers education and secondary schools are a match made in heaven. They are a melting pot where students from an array of smaller primary schools are thrown together in a colossal exposure to social and chronological hierarchies. Mixed in with a vast array of new subjects and teachers. If this isn't a crash course into the world of adulthood, then who knows what else is? It is incredibly easy for adults to take this fact for granted. It is, after all, one of the great landmarks that must be reached in order to enter adulthood.

Students will need to be supported as they navigate through this new environment; there will be several aspects of education that they will be familiar with – lessons and daily structure, for example. However, the concept that they are heading into the final straight before they begin their transition into adulthood and the first tastes of educational autonomy will be brand new. It must not be taken for granted. Capitalising on this new world they find themselves in, careers education must be incorporated from the get-go. Giving students a central focus that will seed the next five years of their life, providing context and focus to underpin their secondary journey.

At its heart, this is what careers education is here for, it weaves its way through every aspect of school life, shining light on everything a student will experience. It gives context and meaning to what could otherwise be a very artificial and sterile environment. A secondary school without a careers programme that prepares students for a dynamic and unknown future is only doing half a job.

There has been a growing awareness of the significance of career education in secondary schools. Thankfully, it is no longer a recommendation of good practice; it has become part of most schools' bread and butter. It has begun to seep into legislation with each year heralding in a new requirement or piece of statutory guidance that schools need to incorporate into their practice. While this is undoubtedly good news, over time it has the potential to become a cursed chalice. While it ensures schools give careers education the significance that it deserves, it can also force it to become bolted on as an extra. Like anything that is repeatedly bolted on, the chances of it becoming perfunctory or simply falling off is non-zero and therefore inevitable before too long.

Tapping on a programme runs the risk of becoming overwhelming and falling apart when stress-tested. Effectively integrating a programme has the power to become self-perpetuating and adaptive when external, or internal, pressures are applied. This is not always as simple as it seems. How do you build a self-propagating system that maintains up-to-date and relevant delivery while requiring minimal industry-specific knowledge? How can this system be delivered by subject matter experts rather than by specialists in careers education?

As will become apparent, just as we emphasise skills over knowledge for students, staff who are equipped with the right skills to support their teaching will be more resilient. They are also more likely to adopt a careers-related focus in their classroom practice. This is what enables integrated careers programmes to succeed and remain adaptive over prolonged periods of time.

7 | Starting strong: Career foundations in secondary school

Summary points

Knowing and Uncovering Your Students' Backgrounds

Understanding a student's primary school experiences helps create a smoother transition to secondary school, especially when supporting the making of connections with a new school's values.

Reframe Questions for Richer Responses

Develop different approaches to speaking to students about school values, by understanding how previous schools' values align with yours to begin to bridge the gap during a period of transition.

Articulation of Simple, Meaningful Values

Clear, simple values allow students and staff to form personal connections with them and to work towards a cohesive and welcoming school community.

Knowing where your students have come from is step one of any "good teacher handbook". Every lesson starts with it. Seriously, if you don't know their story leading to their start with you at secondary school, take the time to explore this avenue sooner rather than later. Primary schools spend a huge amount of time building student character. They are often smaller in student numbers and have the time to tailor the learning specifically to the learner and build incredibly strong relationships with them as a result. Discovering the nuances that each of your feeder primaries develops in their students before they reach you is key. It will enable you to create a transition programme that capitalises on the vast array of experiences they bring with them.

Learning point

A new cohort arrives in September at the start of the academic year. You deliver your introductory assembly/tutor session/ PSH(C)E lesson, and you ask students to give an example of how they have experienced or embodied one of your school values. Let's say "resilience". This is a fairly common task which seeks to help students find a sense of belonging with a new school and its new set of values.

For some, let's call them group A, this might be a very straightforward response. In all likelihood, it will have been part of the language used in their primary school. Of this group, some may give very explicit examples, such as a personal experience or an event from their lives.

For others in group B, there may be more subtle in their response. Giving less tangible examples such as explaining how they might use it in their schooling or home lives or if they think it is a strength of theirs or not.

Group C might be able to define the word or concept and give generic or basic examples of it. But are unable to articulate it within the context of their own lives or schooling.

And group D will be your students for whom this would be an alien concept to which they cannot contribute. Thankfully though, through the increased work done on personal development in primary schools, this group is becoming smaller and smaller.

What causes the variation in response? It might be easy to say that some students are more articulate or have greater knowledge and grasp of language. While this might be true, experience has shown differently. Generally speaking, the students in each of these camps tend to have come from the same primary schools, or group of schools. They will have had previous experience in the articulation of these themes as a result. This is not to suggest that a student's group reflects the quality of their previous school. Rather, it indicates how closely their school's values or personal development programmes align with the values posed in the original question by their new school.

Knowing a little of the history of where the students have come from before joining your school, you are able to build from an existing foundation. Supporting the incorporation into your school's ethos and your own skills integrated curriculum.

7 | Starting Strong: Career Foundations in Secondary School

Rather than starting with your school values, start with theirs. Prime them to start thinking about school beyond the curriculum by recalling where they have come from and then get them to start building their own bridges to their new settings and contexts.

> "The first of our school values is 'resilience'; this is *insert your own definition here*. We believe it is important because *insert your own reason here*. Which one of your previous school's values most closely matches this? Why have you chosen this one? Can you give an example?"
>
> Something as simple as rephrasing and slightly redirecting the question can lead to a richer variety of responses from students. It also helps them begin to find their own path towards belonging in a new school.

Establishing the foundation of learning is crucial when a student enters their new secondary school; every school has its own process. Furthermore, so does every teacher. Inevitably these will focus on one or all of a couple of key themes:

- a rigorous, idealised expectation of behaviour;
- a foundation in academic excellence;
- an expectation to give complete effort in everything they do.

These are fine. They are actually pretty important for students to build a sense of belonging and understand the role they play in a new school. But they are not always realistic, it is a clear example of square peg, round hole.

There will be students who see these expectations as orders or instructions which they might disagree with. You might be able to put forward a convincing argument or set a state of martial law to bring everyone in line, but the foundations of it are not set in the true value of the reason students are in school: to prepare themselves for the future and adulthood.

The long-term ambition of any school leader is to have a common language of learning that doesn't involve any of these statements, that they simply become part of the school's day-to-day business. But in order for this to happen, they cannot be told that it is expected of them. It must be implied in every one of their interactions throughout the school day and experienced in every classroom. Demonstrated by the staff that greet them at the gate, that stand at the front of the room or pick them up in the corridor between lessons. There is nothing more explicit than the implicit.

Understanding what your school ethos or vision means beyond the obvious might seem, well, obvious, but you will be surprised just how much variation there can be in its interpretation by staff and students alike. Broadly speaking they can be interpreted into one (or more) of several categories:

Personal development

How does it relate to the development of the individual? Does it promote personal qualities or ideas which will help them in the world beyond education?

Your approach brings out qualities such as resilience, adaptability, and critical thinking preparing students to life beyond education. There is a focus on fostering self-awareness, community, and critical thinking. Students develop confidence in their own ability and skills to navigate their futures.

Academic progression

How does highlighting hard work and self-discipline apply to more than just achieving high grades in subjects? What "lessons" (pardon the pun?) are students experiencing due to the school's values and ethos?

Your focus is on hard work and self-discipline to not only achieve academically but to also instil perseverance, time management and taking responsibility for oneself. Students develop an appreciation for lifelong learning and are equipped with the essential skills to succeed in any field.

Attitudes and mentality

How does it guide students when faced with new situations or coming up against potential setbacks? How do students articulate their ability to demonstrate this, both in the classroom and in their everyday experiences?

You encourage students to approach new situations with confidence and a problem-solving mindset to equip them to overcome setbacks with resilience. Students are supported in the communication of self and ability to prove themselves in professional and personal pursuits.

Building community

How do they bring students together and give a shared sense of belonging? Do they highlight the importance of being a productive member of the community? Or the skills and qualities that it takes to take on a meaningful role within it? With the advent of social media and online communities, this can sometimes feel artificial if not truly genuine and embraced.

You pride yourselves on your school community and the feeling of belonging it brings to staff and students through a shared purpose. Students are emphasised on the importance of teamwork and leadership, through this they gain the skills necessary to contribute meaningfully to society.

Meaningful relationships

How does it encourage students to build meaningful and mutually respectful relationships with those around them? Does it highlight the importance of a social and professional network to exist within?

Your school is built around mutual respect and empathy for one's peers, helping students build strong personal and professional relationships. Trust and communication play a central role in student life to foster the development of positive interactions both within and beyond school life.

The ethos and values of a school will always be unique in each setting. However, for them to have a long-term resonance with students, there must be an understanding of them outside of the school. They must act to prepare students for life outside of education, otherwise they are simply a set of rules which must be abided by in the school. There is no better way to have something ignored by a teenager, than to tell them they must do it without reason or meaning.

STAFF SUPPORT RESOURCE

Articulation of a school's ethos and values.

Being able to articulate the school's ethos and values supports school leaders in building a cohesive and welcoming community for staff and newly arriving students. It is not enough for it to remain here, this level of articulation and understanding needs to extend across the entire staffing of the school and through each and every cohort of students.

> As you would with students, so too should you with staff. For values to be valued they must be embraced by everyone, including staff. So often it is looked over, or just briefly referred to in staff inductions of September insets, but it needs to have the time it deserves. You cannot expect students to live them if the staff can barely reference them.
>
> The most effective messages are the simplest, not because they are easy to recall, but because they allow everyone to imprint onto it their own experiences and interpretations to build a personal connection with it. Someone with a personal connection to something is far more likely to stick with it through the thick and thin and embody it in more of what they do.
>
> It doesn't take much; it doesn't need to be rammed down their ears or have hours spent over consecutive weeks; it doesn't even need to take up valuable Continuing Professional Development (CPD) time. It just needs recognition and tangible examples scattered throughout: weekly reference during staff briefing, recognition awards, or examples shared over the course of a term, even inviting open discussions as to how they can be better demonstrated through the school. Constant low-level repetition is so much more effective at building value into values than big expressions once a year.

Action checklist

- ☑ Choose one of your main feeder primary schools. If possible, book a brief call or meeting with a contact teacher there. Ask them specifically about their school's values or personal development programmes and how they are communicated to students.
  Think: understanding student starting points.

- ☑ In an upcoming tutor time or PSHE session with your Year 7 students, explicitly connect your secondary school's values to the values they may have already learnt in primary school. Use a bridging question like the example in the chapter: "Our school value is "Resilience"... Which value from your primary school is most similar to this? Why? Can you give an example?".
  Think: building bridges, not blank slates.

7| Starting Strong: Career Foundations in Secondary School

- [✓] Take one of your school's stated values or ethos statements. Spend 15 minutes reflecting on what this value truly means beyond the official definition. Consider: How does it link to personal development? Academic success? Student attitudes? Community building? Meaningful relationships?
Think: values with depth, not just slogans.

8 | Moving beyond "because I said so": Purposeful careers learning

Summary points

Challenging Outdated Education Norms

Prepare students for the real world, beyond the classroom, by understanding the "why" behind their learning, moving away from the "because I said so" approach in an evolution from the largely unchanged education system of the past 150 years.

Reframing Education for Career Readiness

Focusing on integrating career learning into the curriculum by showing students how each subject connects to real-world skills, developing a deeper understanding of, and appreciation for, their lessons and relevance to their future careers.

Bridging Classroom Learning and Future Careers

Practical examples demonstrating to support students in realising, and understanding, that education isn't just about academics, but about developing transferable skills that are critical for success in any career.

The educational system, secondary in particular, has remained largely unchanged for over 150 years. It can be described as a "because I said so" system whereby students are expected to follow certain processes and procedures because this is how it ran last year and the year before that. In the short term, this works perfectly well. In the short term, there is little need for change, and it will set a strong legacy. But over time this becomes more and more outdated with each passing year. Expecting students to behave in a certain way based on the fact that this is what everyone else has done, and then dictating this to them on day one with the reason being "because this is how we do it here", does not set the true expectation of learners in education. Instead, it reinforces conformity over understanding, and misses the opportunity to engage students in the why behind the behaviours we value.

The three points of a school's educational foundation referred to previously are a prime example of a "because I said so system". Readdressing them, now with a careers learning focus superimposed onto it might look like the following:

1. A rigorous idealised expectation of behaviour
   - Evidencing this for students with the reasons why society, and therefore they personally, need to demonstrate common decency to one another in order to be able to function in their future careers is key. For some, this realisation does not come as easily as it does to others. This is where the school's behaviour policies come in, they should be there to support students in such a way as to prepare, not dictate.
2. A foundation in academic excellence
   - This is a tough one, which will be delved into further later in this chapter. But for students to be told that the purpose of education is to achieve academic excellence is outdated and simply wrong. If the education system is to remain fit for purpose, then it must change and evolve to meet the needs of the communities it serves. While academic excellence is very impressive and undoubtedly an achievement to be celebrated, it is only the reality for some; what about the rest?
3. An expectation to give complete effort in everything they do
   - Within this, there needs to be an understanding that we are all human. There is a need for students to learn to self-regulate and prepare them to understand the importance of a work-life balance. It is vital that schools support students with the management of expectations and enable them to understand that it is okay not to be streamlined and perfect 100% of the time.

In all cases, as will become apparent, it simply isn't enough that students are told to learn; they must be supported in understanding why they are learning and take an active role in it. There needs to be a learning cycle of acquisition, application, and recall.

This shouldn't be new information for anyone reading this. It has been thoroughly researched and evaluated many times over; people have, ironically or not, dedicated their lives to it. Learning requires repetition. To master a concept, time must be spent reviewing, practising, assessing, and reapplying in a multitude of different contexts. This is as much true of learning a musical instrument as it is of developing a sense of self. Even finding one's place in a school and hence a career. This is a concept that is incredibly well understood by schools but is often overlooked in the most fundamental of opportunities. Why is much of career-related learning fixated on a passive, information-delivery-driven approach, which, as is now well known, is not effective?

The long and short of it is that much of what is considered careers-related learning is still held under the common misconception that careers learning is about job learning. That, in order for a student to be able to find "career success", they need to be asked what their favourite subject is and then list of jobs that relate to that field. At its best, this model is career limiting. Pigeonholing a student into a particular way of thinking about themselves as someone who is only academically driven in a particular field, to the exclusion of all others. Great if you are the desired subject teacher, terrible if you are not. Is it any wonder why one of the toughest classes to teach are the Year 9 "options" subjects towards the end of the summer term. Students with the mindset of I am no longer studying this subject because I do not want to work in this field when I am older, see no benefit in learning within the lessons, goodwill will only get you so far.

Learning point

A student is in attendance at a parents' evening with their parents. They sit down in front of their science teacher. The teacher is very supportive and has nothing but high praise for this student. However, they are not achieving their full potential. All parties are very aware of this fact and while the student is good at science, biology in particular, they are not that particularly interested in science. They are actually quite bored and uninspired by the content of most lessons.

This science teacher explains to them they have "natural aptitude" for science and would make a very successful biochemist or even a marine biologist. Hoping to inspire them to commit to their subject. Understandably by showing them the potential that a successful grade would unlock in their futures.

Following this parents' evening, there is no change in the students grade. If anything there is a slight decline, and their general engagement begins to fall.

It is not fair to say the teacher in this situation acted incorrectly. They saw the potential in one of their students and, being passionate about their subject, wanted to instil the same love and drive that they have for it into them. However, this was not the case. It caused the opposite effect: the student was uninterested in where this subject was leading, and therefore its perceived value decreased. While this is a somewhat extreme and abbreviated example, it is an all too common scenario that crops up. It might not explicitly be during a parents' evening, but these conversations are happening nonetheless.

It is these conversations that lead to the classic trope that is heard by teachers up and down the country day in and day out. When teachers speak to anyone outside of education, it is almost boasted as it is proudly proclaimed to them, "not once have I ever needed to remember what photosynthesis is". Congratulations, the entire educational system thanks you for your honesty. You should be very proud of yourself.

How can they be to blame for this? They were told at the time that this series of definitions or equations needed to be learnt, and so they were, sometimes even without question and for what end? They were right. They most likely never did need to know it again, but does that mean they shouldn't have learnt it in the first place?

Separating the subject from the lesson is counter-intuitive and often quite an alien concept for students and teachers alike. But in order to change this narrative, it is crucial. The lesson is the tool by which the subject is taught. The subject is the knowledge, and the context in which the medium of the lesson is delivered. The lesson is what students will carry with them throughout their education and into their lives, it is the lessons which they will use on a daily basis in their careers and personal lives; the subject is simply how it is introduced in the first place.

> Coming back to the initial scenario, changing the perspective, or shifting the angle of engagement with the student away from the subject and towards the lesson has the potential to change the dynamics of the student's relationship with education. Rather than highlighting jobs the student could do if they were academically excellent within science, consider a different approach. Focus instead on why the subject is not just important but also enhancing for their futures.
>
> Highlighting to the student and their parents the attributes they have demonstrated during lesson time, and explaining why these skills have a far-reaching and measurable impact on their lives, is key. This begins to help separate the lessons from the subject itself. The subjects are specific; the lessons are universal

Teachers are subject specialists. They are English, maths, geography, PE specialists; they are not careers specialists. This is not to point a finger of blame, but to state a simple fact. Teachers are specialists, people who are artfully skilled in imparting their disciplinary knowledge on young people. Careers learning, however, is not their area of expertise. Nor is it expected that they should be. They are however the ones in the greatest position to signpost students to the importance and significance that their subject holds in the world, away from the academic and classroom constraints.

8| Moving Beyond "Because I Said So": Purposeful Careers Learning

> **IN-CLASS RESOURCE**
>
> Using a variety of techniques and approaches means that all students will have the opportunity to engage with it on their terms.
>
> There are lots of different ways that in which careers learning can be drip fed to students; little and often is what is needed, not intensive crash courses.
>
> ### Job signposting
>
> Raising awareness and job advertising to students has its place, to put it simply, "you cannot be what you cannot see". This doesn't mean telling them about every job that exists in your field. Where possible, highlight the importance and significance of the local and national landscape in reaction to the curriculum-specific subjects.
>
> ### Direct links
>
> Link each learning point/lesson/topic to a specific job or industry. Including a bio or profile to bookend the applied period of learning will provide context of learning in terms of the world beyond education and the big picture at play. Ensure that this is not delivered in a limiting way, such that it gives the impression that the only route possible from the chosen theme is this particular pathway. There is no better way to disengage a learner than tell them it applies to something they couldn't care less about; it isn't inspiring, it's misjudged.
>
> ### Self-discovery
>
> Tasking students with exploring the job market and discovering related careers to particular topics or themes from lessons is important. The trick is to be persistent, consistent and supportive in its long-term delivery. Inevitably it will take time to implement the routine into lessons. However, as with all consistent approaches in classrooms, the routine soon kicks in and will become second nature. It could take on the role of the introductory lesson where students are asked to predict their learning and create their own point of reference for the duration of that particular topic.
>
> ### Revision/topic summaries
>
> Revision, let's face it, is tedious. It serves one of two purposes: either to prepare for an exam or to consolidate the learning over a particular period of time. So often these blur into one and result in mind mapping, exam practice, or revision maps. This does not spark a love of education for most students. Asking them

instead to summarise their learning in relation to the research of different jobs/careers/industries that utilise the knowledge and skills developed in this period of learning. It's like the spoonful of sugar that helps the medicine become more palatable. This one in particular can be planned for in advance and built directly into a curriculum and sequencing of lessons. Once made, its template is very easily adapted and transferred, even between subjects.

Bring someone in

Everyone knows someone; there are a vast number of ways in which external guests can be utilised in a careers programme. One of the simplest, yet potentially the most impactful, is for a teacher to bring in a guest from their industry and ask them to contribute to a 10–15 section of one of their lessons. This doesn't need to be for the whole cohort, it can be for a single class; in terms of planning and preparation, this is the simplest of options. The trick to its effectiveness lies in the numbers. If every teacher organised one of these a term, the result could be each student having up to 100 opportunities to see an application of education in action in a single year!

STAFF SUPPORT RESOURCE

Each subject has its own deeper meaning; getting staff, and therefore students, to find them and talk about them is what's important.

Maths:

Maths isn't just about numbers; it's about solving problems through systematic application of processes. It is about thinking critically and taking a clinical approach in breaking down complex tasks into manageable chunks.

- Problem-solving
- Critical thinking
- Pattern recognition
- Logical and non-verbal reasoning

English:

Isn't just about writing reams of text or analysing someone else's work; it's about finding beauty and deriving meaning in the world. It is about being creative and improving their communication of emotion and empathy through their words.

- Communication
- Empathy
- Critical analysis
- Creativity

Science:

Isn't just about remembering a colossal number of facts relating to the natural world; it is about taking nothing at face value and questioning the information that you are being provided with. It is about posing a point or opinion and working through the steps to prove and justify it.

- Scientific inquiry
- Evidence-based reasoning
- Experimentation
- Methodical problem-solving

Art and Design:

Isn't just about being a good artist; it is about seeing the beauty in nature and taking time to transform imagination into a tangible outcome. It is about collecting a skillset over time and applying it in creative and unique ways.

- Visual communication
- Collaboration
- Creativity
- Problem-solving

Business Studies:

Isn't just about listening to stories of how business owners created and ran their companies; it is about gaining an appreciation for the nuance of developing and bringing a product to market and building a business to facilitate it. It is about building confidence in the complexities of decision-making that has farther reaching consequences than the individual who made them.

- Financial literacy
- Leadership
- Decision-making
- Analytical thinking

Computer Science:

Isn't just about learning to code and working out how the internet works; it is about using rational systematic lines of reasoning to create a desired output to solve specific problems. It is about finding creative solutions to problems which have not yet been proposed or even realised.

- Creative problem-solving
- Logical reasoning
- Technical literacy
- Collaboration

Drama:

Isn't just about becoming an actor destined for film and stage; it is about understanding that things don't need to be perfect, that life is fluid and improvised. It is about reading into the expressions and intentions of people you meet and learning to work with them, regardless of similarities or differences.

- Improvisation and adaptability
- Communication
- Empathy
- Teamwork

Design Technologies:

Isn't just about drawing and making things using physical dexterity; it is about planning, developing and prototyping based on set criteria. It is about thinking on your feet, using resources at hand to synthesise creative solutions to physical problems.

- Innovation
- Technical analysis
- Project management
- Critical thinking

Geography:

Isn't just about learning about different countries and their socio-economic identities; it is about understanding the sensitivity of cultures different to your own. It is about realising your position in the local, national, and international communities and gaining an appreciation for the natural world around you.

- Data analysis
- Cultural sensitivity
- Environmental literacy
- Research techniques

History:

Isn't just about recalling the events of the past; it is about understanding the context in which learning takes place. It is about critically analysing events and understanding the patterns found in the consequences of actions and the far-reaching impacts of these, across time and geography.

- Contextual understanding
- Decision-making
- Empathy
- Critical analysis

Modern Foreign Languages:

Isn't just about learning a new language, which potentially may not be used again; it is about cultivating a cultural identity and understanding cultures that are similar yet different to your own. It is about seeing the importance in application of memory and adaptability in a highly dynamic world and workplace.

- Communication
- Cultural awareness
- Memory development
- Adaptability

Music:

Isn't just about learning to play an instrument or being able to read sheet music; it is about fostering emotional intelligence and creative freedom, regardless of its medium. It is about mastering the art of treading the fine line between discipline and mastery and creative collaboration.

- Creativity
- Collaboration
- Emotional intelligence
- Discipline

Physical Education:

Isn't just about enjoying sport or being part of the netball or football teams; it is about strategic and empowering leadership and teamwork. It is about understanding that the sum of a team's parts is less than its whole and knowing who to trust at moments when it counts most.

- Teamwork
- Self-discipline
- Stress management
- Goal setting and achievement

> **Religious Education:**
>
> Isn't just about learning the histories and customs of worldwide religions; it is about understanding and empathising with different cultural and religious points of view. It is about taking time to reflect on personal priorities and one's place in the world as well as finding your own spiritual journey.
>
> - Critical thinking
> - Ethical reasoning
> - Empathy
> - Social responsibility

Action checklist

- [x] Before planning your next lesson, pause and ask yourself: "If a student asked me 'Why are we learning this?', beyond just the exam, what meaningful, real-world answer could I give?" Use these to start your lesson and frame the learning.
Think: purposeful lesson framing.

- [x] Choose one core skill that your subject develops (e.g. problem-solving, communication, analysis). Imagine you have 30 seconds in an elevator to "sell" the value of this skill to a student who doubts its relevance. Write down your "elevator pitch"; keep it concise, compelling, and focused on transferable skills, not just subject knowledge.
Think: skills-focused communication.

- [x] Choose a lesson you taught recently. Look back at your lesson plan or resources. Can you identify at least two explicit links to real-world applications, careers, or transferable skills that you could have highlighted more strongly during the lesson? Note these down as "missed opportunities" and consider how you could incorporate them next time you teach that lesson.
Think: retroactive relevance-finding.

9 | Why teach? Why learn? Careers and purpose

Summary points

Challenging Traditional Views of Teaching

Encourage teachers to consider broader benchmarks for student success, such as personal growth, resilience, and life skills. Challenge teachers to reframe how they measure their impact and articulate this with one another.

Understanding and Articulating the Deeper Meaning of Schools

Support students and teachers in reflecting on their interactions with the education system and where they fit into it, personally and professionally. Question and communicate curriculum choices, assessment, and the role schools play in students' future lives.

Promoting Reflection and Personal Growth with Students and Staff

Practical activities that can be used to help both teachers and students reflect on their motivations and goals to develop a deeper understanding of education.

Ask a teacher why they teach, or why they are in education, and you will receive a multitude of different answers. These include, but are certainly not limited to, the possibility that they were inspired by a teacher when they were younger and wanted to follow in those footsteps. Or perhaps they find their subject truly fascinating and feel compelled to share that passion with a new generation. They hope to inspire their students to pursue the field themselves one day. Both of these are very noble, absolutely valid, reasons to become a teacher or to work in education. However, they hold a fundamental flaw, and that is, if they have not achieved either of these two targets, they have failed – failed themselves and the students they serve, which is also obviously incorrect. Just because you haven't inspired a student to follow in your footsteps or to engage with a career that links to your subject's content, does not mean you have failed. So either their motives are wrong or there is a deeper meaning to their career as a teacher.

> **Learning point**
>
> Ask a group of teachers why they teach, ask for a quick decision, but be specific about what made them choose to become a teacher. The answers most likely fall into one of two broad categories: a love of subject or a want to change the future of young people.
>
> **Of those who chose the subject:**
>
> Ask them why that particular subject? Why have they chosen to be specialists in their subject? There will be a variety of answers again, but this should start to engage a more passionate level of thinking and the answers that come with it.
>
> Ask them how much of their passion for the subject is actually related to the curriculum they teach? And how explicit are they in their teaching? Hopefully, by this point you have started to break down some of the initial resistance and made first steps towards chipping away at the obvious and are getting into the realities of it.
>
> Continue to probe further: "You are clearly passionate about your subject, why do you not work in this industry and apply it on a daily basis, why are you in school?" This often comes back with responses around wanting to inspire their students or share their passion, in addition to their love of the subject.
>
> At the end of the day, schools are student-centred regardless of any other factor.
>
> **Of those who chose to change the future:**
>
> It is now their time to face the inquisition. Ask them why they have chosen to teach that particular subject. Why not offer general support to students, as a youth worker/leader or part of a youth engagement club? Why have they chosen a subject in a school?
>
> It will likely come down to whether it is something that they enjoy or that they are academically good at, probably from school and therefore into university. Don't stop there; continue the line of questioning; just because *you* enjoy that subject, does it really make it relevant, or enjoyable, to every student? How can you change the future of a child in your subject if they don't enjoy it or are disengaged?

In both of these cases, the line of questioning leads in similar directions with similar outcomes, often resulting in teachers beginning to question their practice and finding ways to justify their opinions. (Stop them before they get to this point: it could end poorly and result in a

9| Why Teach? Why Learn? Careers and Purpose

recruitment problem on the horizon.) But this is not necessary at all; there is no need for justification. Teaching is paradoxical; it's time to embrace it. You have dedicated your career, adult professional life, to support young people to be able to transition into adulthood to fulfil their adult lives. Most likely jobs or careers that have no translation to the content of the lessons you taught them in the first place. This is amazing! Let's now turn it into a force for good.

> Taking the spotlight slightly away from teaching itself, ask your audience: What is the purpose of a school? Further still, why have their subjects been chosen as curriculum landmarks? Why German over French (or vice versa)? Why Citizenship over Politics? Digging deeper, why is the content of their curriculum such that it is? It surely can't encompass everything there is to know about that subject? Surely it doesn't even scratch the surface? Why, then, have certain aspects been kept while others removed? This can't surely be the work of the exam board, as they will write any old test based on the content of the curriculum? So why?

Now this is a lot of questions to throw at a room. However, as will become apparent, the nature of, and answers to, these questions are largely irrelevant. The journey in which they take your train of thought is far more valuable and informative. It starts to ask teachers to begin thinking about the path a student takes through a school, both physical and metaphorical, not just the journey within their classroom.

Other than the superficially obvious, there has been very little change to the educational system since the 1870s. A system whereby students, regardless of personal circumstance or background, are subjected to the exact same series of standards set out by a community of academics. Either it is glorified day care, or it is something deeper. That is not to say there is any ill intention by those that decreed and continued its tradition. Round holes and square pegs surely come to mind? This is a system built by the experiences of the 1% and delivered to 99%.

Reminding staff that, for better or worse, they are part of this system is a little depressing; no matter how dynamic and forward-thinking their teaching might be, every teacher will see an element of their own practice reflected in this. Not all is lost, there are a final set of questions, from which the answers should begin to drip forward which will help reframe their practice, teaching, and planning. Now is the time to bring forward a mini revolution in the classroom and the provision the school is putting in place for their students.

Start by reposing the "why do schools exist?" question with a slight twist. What is the purpose of school? What are we actually preparing them for? This will likely result in answers to the effect of: "to help raise rounded individuals who function in society" and "to give them a bright, autonomous future without limit or expectation". If this is true and we really are preparing them for the next steps or adulthood, then why do school league tables exist? Why do we worry about Progress 8 scores and The English Baccalaureate (EBACC) uptake percentages? Why are schools and teachers, nationally and internally, held to account for the scores a student gains on an arbitrary assessment?

 Author's note

This actually can be a powerful question to introduce to students. However, it is not without its risk: the context which it is asked in, the emotional state of the recipient, and the tone in which it's asked will all elicit different responses, some of which may not be the intended outcome.

Teacher: So, why are you in school?
Student: Honestly? Because I have to be.
T: That's a pretty rough way to spend your childhood, don't you think?
S: Yeah, kind of.
T: I mean, it's a lot of time to spend on something just because someone says you have to.
S: And?
T: Look, you're here whether you like it or not, right? So don't let it go to waste. Besides the GCSEs, what else are you actually getting out of this place? When you leave with your GCSEs, what else will you have to show for all this time?
S: I dunno, what's the point if it's just about getting grades?
T: The grades open doors, sure, but what you learn along the way is what helps you walk through them. They aren't the easiest thing for everyone, and they can feel like the whole point of school. But they're not the only thing that matters.
S: Then what's the point? I'm not gonna get them anyway.
T: Maybe. But what you're doing here isn't just about grades. It's about figuring out how to deal with life. Stuff like showing up, working through challenges, even when it feels hard. Those are skills you'll need no matter where you go or what you do.
S: Doesn't feel like it.

> T: But imagine you leave here and get a job; what kind of person are they going to want? Someone who gives up, or someone who gives it a go, even when it's hard?
> S: I dunno. Probably someone who tries.
> T: And school is where you start that mentality. Even if it's not about the grades, just showing up, trying, learning from mistakes, that's what will make the difference. You're not just working for today's exams; you're building yourself for what's next.
> S: I guess, but I'm just bad at it.
> T: Everyone's got stuff they're bad at, and school's where you figure that out too. What if instead of worrying about being perfect, you just tried a little? Start small, one thing at a time. You don't have to be the best; you just have to keep showing up.
>
> A little staged, yes, but the start of this conversation is happening every day in classrooms up and down the country. How they develop and conclude can make or break a student's engagement with education. At the end of the day, it isn't only about grades, it is about helping guide the young person to their brightest possible future.

> Now it is time to bring it back together; it's time to ask teaching staff why they teach their subjects again. This time tell them they need to convince someone from outside of their subject to convert to join their department. If they can't convince a "willing" colleague, what chance do they stand with a *insert expletive here* teenager – a little harsh, yes, but valid. Many students will be in the position of that second teacher. They will already know they prefer another subject and will need "convincing" that your subject is worth their investment.
>
> The most persuasive arguments will be those who are able to articulate the beauty of their subject beyond the obvious, beyond the exam, beyond the curriculum. If you can convince and show a student the purpose of your subject, you have done so much more than just inspire them to work.
>
> The teachers in front of you must not leave this discussion and intellectual journey in the room; they need to take this with them and into their classrooms. Don't let them forget what happened on this day.

After all, teaching is a highly glorified sales job; teachers are, each and every day, selling education to students. The students who buy into their education are the ones who receive most from it. It's time to get selling!

So set the tone for everything that follows; it is going to be impossible to disregard national curriculums and standardised assessments, these have become institutionalised and form the bedrock of what most schools are built upon. It is time to ask the question again.

> "Why are you a teacher?"
>
> If they've engaged with this line of reasoning and have truly caught onto it, they should now find it significantly harder to give their reason. They'll be caught between two things: what they know to be true, the current state of affairs, and what they feel to be true, the beauty they see in their subjects.

Working with teaching staff to find their inner drive and cause for teaching is no easy task; unfortunately, there is no golden rule that can be followed or a silver bullet for a sure-fire kill. For each and every one, their drive is unique and personal and they need to find it for themselves. Lines of questioning like this help to crack open the door to this and starts to cast light down.

IN-CLASS RESOURCE

Self-reflection activities for students to encourage them to find and connect with their own meaning in education.

"The purpose of education" student reflection activities

These activities can be used to support and encourage students to reflect on their education and their relationship with it. Much like teaching staff, students who understand the purpose behind it are far more likely to engage meaningfully. When they do, it becomes something that serves their goals and supports their own objectives and outcomes.

The following activities are designed to fit into the short time usually allocated for tutor times, registration periods, or personal development sessions.

They are short, hands-on, and easily adaptable.

Timelining

Running from their earliest memory through to the present day, challenge students to place a positive, decisive, or pivotal memory or experience above the line. Below the line, something that didn't go to plan, depending on the group of students, this could be framed as negative experiences. Aim to have one of each for each academic year that they have gone through. This may not come naturally to many students. You might need to offer some modelling based on your own experiences. You could also suggest a few simple themes they might want to explore. Just be careful not to influence or lead their responses.

The second pass over this timeline asks them to further populate it with the perceived impact it has had on them and the moment they find themselves in now. This second pass is much harder to achieve and will almost certainly require encouragement and support in order for honest and committed additions. Reassuring students that these are private reflections and do not need to be publicly shared can aid in the committing of personal or emotional content to paper.

This could stop at the second pass, used to show how all of our choices and encounters, good or bad, have led to this point now. Some have made it easier, some harder, but all to here. Or it can go one final step further: getting the students to identify what led to these encounters/opportunities and how they can best learn from them to manufacture similar encounters in the future. Knowing, with hindsight, how you got somewhere is one thing; orchestrating it to happen again is another.

Letters to themselves

This can often feel awkward for students to conduct activities like this; encouragement and an atmosphere of no fear and no bad answers can often subside this and allow them to think more deeply on their task.

Past-self: getting students to write letters to their past-self is a good exercise in reflection, in particular in their journeys so far. Justifying the choices they made and understanding where their previous decisions have led them to. So often we talk about the consequences of actions, but rarely does this focus on the historical actions taken and how these have influenced the person they have become.

Future-self: a slightly more traditional activity to carry out with students, particularly when they are at key transition points in their education. However, varying the timeframe in which they need to be addressed can lead to some interesting revelations and highlight the significance of target setting and holding oneself accountable to oneself. Starting with short time frames between writing and reading of one to two weeks allows students to reflect on their short-term targets and outcomes. This timeframe can be stepped up to more significant timeframes of months, terms, or even years. As they progress through, they will begin to reflect on their own ambitions and the reality of their ability to not just set achievable targets, but also meaningful ones.

Metaphormisation [*sic*]

Education is like… (yes, this is the start of a simile, but you try to find an obviously metaphor-ey sentence starter. Yes, you're right, this section could have been called simile-inating, but clearly that doesn't read as well.)

Challenge students to complete the sentence starter of "Education is like…" or "School is like…" This will always generate your standard answers of "prison", "marathon", or something borderline offensive. Obviously give them the time they deserve, but push past it. Really it is about getting students to critically engage with the principle of it and justify their answers. The wilder the range, the better. Other than generating humour, this will require students to think about education and schools from alternative perspectives.

The big debate

Grouping students into small teams, with no more than three in each, can be eye-opening. Ask them to put forward their own arguments about the purpose of education and the teaching profession. This works especially well when they are given the freedom to speak openly and not hold back. Offering guidance or suggesting themes that they might want to explore can serve to scaffold their arguments; however, for this to be most effective, it must be their own views. Where possible, limit the use of internet access or completing as part of a project that involves homework.

These can be delivered as an essay, speech, TED (style) talk, or as a blog-style recording. While great options for students to explore their creativity and record their work in a manner that suits them. Turning their research into a dialogue can be much more entertaining and lead to interesting and often unexpected insights for the teachers, just as much as the students. Using a basic debating structure is a reliable and well-tested approach. This can include opening statements, primary arguments, opening the floor for discussion, and closing statements. There are plenty of resources available online to help implement this routine.

> Asking students to justify their personal beliefs helps them build a deeper connection to their own personal philosophy. This becomes especially powerful when they are faced with challenging questions and opposing opinions. It can be tough, but it is absolutely worth the effort. The benefits of tasks like this go far beyond the initial goal of self-discovery. They also support the development of self-efficacy, logical debate, and the linguistic dexterity needed for strong verbal reasoning.

Action checklist

- [x] Take 10 minutes for personal reflection. Ask yourself: "Beyond the curriculum and exam results, why do I really teach?" Note down your honest answer, what motivates you, what impact do you hope to have, what deeper meaning do you find in teaching? This is for your reflection, not to be shared unless you choose.
  Think: reconnecting with your teaching purpose.

- [x] In an upcoming tutor group or PSHE session, pose the question to your students: "What is the purpose of school for you?" Facilitate an open and honest discussion, listen to their perspectives, even critical ones. Don't judge or correct; just listen and understand.
  Think: understanding students' perspectives on education's purpose.

- [x] In your next department meeting, initiate a discussion around the question: "If exams disappeared tomorrow, what would be the essential purpose and value of our subject?" Create a short, compelling statement that articulates the deeper meaning and lifelong value of your subject. Plan to share these "subject purpose statements" with students.
  Think: redefining subject value beyond assessment.

10 | Beyond exams: Defining the purpose of subjects

Summary points

Breaking the Cycle of Routine

Challenge educators to rethink the purpose of their subjects beyond exams, to start shifting focus from assessment to real-world impact and lifelong learning.

Defining the Purpose of Subjects

Encourage teachers to explore the deeper value of their subjects, creating and sharing explanations that highlight practical applications and lifelong skills, helping students see beyond the obvious.

Rethinking the Standard Curriculum

Support staff to rediscover their passion for teaching, giving time to meaningful conversations that shape a more purposeful education system, which is centred around a core principle of preparing students for the future.

Working in schools can become very formulaic. While there are, in the short term, day-to-day variations and excitements, the long-term, year-on-year repetitions are very much predictable and follow a predictable pattern. There is something comfortable in the timetabled structure to the days, weeks, terms, and even years. This comfort can be reassuring, unlike other industries, yet there are few occasions in one's career where there is a fundamental systematic change and shake up. As a result, there has been very little change to the curriculum and educational system as a whole. Ultimately, it still boils down to delivering knowledge to a student over a period of time and then assessing their ability to remember it at the end. That's about it.

As previously alluded to, being a teacher is more than preparing students to pass an exam. If it was as simple as that, there wouldn't be any need for them in the first place. So what happens when you take the concept of examinations away? What's the point of a school then?

> **Learning point**
>
> With a captive audience (a CPD session or inset, say), there are a couple of questions which will trigger some interesting conversations.
>
> - What purpose does a subject serve if there is no exam at the end of it?
>
> And
>
> - If this was the case, what would the ideal curriculum look like for a subject?
>
> Asking these questions to staff in a school is a way of shifting the focus of their subject away from the academic and towards the practical. It is quite important to note that only a very small number of teachers will have worked in their dedicated subject field outside of education. Yet, every student will study that subject during their time at school.

The answers to these questions can, and should, be shared with students. Showing the human side and sharing the understanding of a sometimes contradictory situation we all find ourselves in, but with a common goal. To get them out at the end of it better educated and prepared for the world that awaits them.

Questioning the purpose of subjects must become more and more relevant if the needs of society are truly going to be met. Particularly from a student's perspective. They will not only help shape the vision of a school-wide careers programme, but also dictate how it is embraced by teaching staff and interpreted by the students at the receiving end. Developing this line of questioning further will help staff find, or indeed re-find, the purpose of their curriculums. It is not about rewriting everything and ignoring exams, but rather about picking out the underlying fundamental elements of subjects.

> Keep questioning, pushing for more answers.
>
> If you had the opportunity to rewrite your curriculum, what would you keep? What would you ditch? What would you bring in? All the while asking "why?" Why have you chosen this? Why have you selected that? Why? Why? Why? Take it further still; why let these questions remain hypothetical? Get them committed to paper and have time spent thinking them through, bring them into conversation with one another. Encourage discussions and collaborations to develop their thoughts.

This next step is very much time dependent. It does not serve to produce any tangible outcomes, granted, but blue-sky and out of the box thinking and allowing staff to indulge in their creativity is important. As far as developing thought processes, though, this is big; it can lead to some interesting conversations and deliver impassioned lessons by empowered teachers when fully embraced.

> With a generic, blank template – nothing more than an empty table – in front of them, ask each department to set out their ideal departmental curriculum. The focus is not on the micro level of individual topics and lessons, but rather the macro, the broad strokes that overarch a curriculum. What should become apparent within the conversations that happen between staff is where they find passion in their subjects, but more importantly, where they see value. When asked to justify decisions, debates will arise around these justifications, in which teachers can start to realise the greater potential of their subjects.

The act of articulation and reasoned thought is one that, as teachers, the profession doesn't dedicate a large amount of time or resources to. Giving, not just time, but actual freedom to express what drives their passion for the subject and where this sits in terms of their daily practice is incredibly powerful and grounding. This can sometimes lead to hard realisations that there is a disconnect with the reality of teaching and the world in which it inhabits.

The temptation with any staff training sessions is to put tight timings on it and restrict conversation to a limited window. While this is highly effective at ensuring that CPD is completed within its allotted time slot so that the next session can start, it is yet another example of an unrealistic and unreflective process of working that is being imposed on education. Give teachers the time to speak, to compare ideas and take a moment to have a real conversation, and let them finish. Equally, encouraging discussion groups to be made of a mixture of teachers with levels of responsibility and to level the playing field. After all it is the ones who have just joined the profession who have the most up-to-date experience of the world outside of the classroom; let them speak. Everyone is an individual and, as a result, everyone will have their own priorities and passions; let them be shared and explored.

> **IN-CLASS RESOURCE**
>
> It isn't just teachers; the students know why they are here too.
>
> The thing is, it doesn't end with staff; students also benefit from finding their own voice and their own purpose. Guiding students to have an appreciation of learning and for all of the benefits it brings, reaches so much further than sitting an exam on a 600 × 600 desk in Year 11 – it can be life-changing.
>
> Use student councils, or student voice, or student leadership, or whatever you call it, to gather anecdotal data from across their peer group. Whatever your view on the significance of student attitude towards education might be, the fact remains that they are ultimately the ones receiving it. In twenty years' time, they will make up the majority of the workforce. Understanding where student perspectives currently stand and getting a sense of the overall landscape will help guide you. It will show you how explicit you need to be when conveying not only the careers programme but also how staff discuss their subjects with students.
>
> Young people aren't particularly subtle, and neither is the approach to gathering their opinions. Often, it is the questions that get straight to the point that deliver the most pragmatic answers.
>
> - How do teachers better prepare you for the future? Examples?
> - Do you understand why each subject is on your timetable?
> - If there weren't any exams, would you still work as hard as you do?
> - If you had the choice, what would you replace GCSEs with?
> - At what point in your education did you most enjoy coming to school? Why? If it isn't now, what is it about now that makes it this way?
>
> The resulting answers to these questions can go on to support the planning and delivery of staff training to better focus on areas which are in most need of development. It also provides feedback which can be used to shine a light on the area and/or staff who are delivering a really meaningful curriculum.

STAFF SUPPORT RESOURCE

Guiding students in the understanding of a subject's place in their lives.

A guide to help staff start off each academic year with a simple slide that goes alongside, or if you're feeling brave, in place of, your "expectations" slide. Setting out the deeper meaning of your subject. Something along the lines of: "These are my expectations of you, these are your expectations of me, these are our expectations of our subject."

English:

English supports you in the mastery of effective and clear communication. It encourages empathy and invites you to explore alternative and sometimes conflicting points of view and gives you the skills to derive meaning and draw conclusions from them.

Maths:

Maths supports you in the ability to see problems as solvable quantities through the use of logical sequencing and reasoned arguments. It enables you to interpret the world logically and helps guide everyday decisions regarding budgeting, time management, and seeking solutions in a methodical manner.

Science:

Science cultivates curiosity and an appreciation for a deeper understanding of the world around us. It teaches critical thinking and the importance of questioning assumptions and not taking life at face value through experimentation and precise observations.

Art and Design:

Art and Design support you in your expressive creation and channeling creativity into tangible outputs which seek to push personal and societal boundaries. It teaches an appreciation for differences and finding meaning in what could otherwise be alien or unknown cultures and aesthetics.

Business Studies:

Business Studies provides you with practical knowledge about the world of enterprise and commerce. It introduces concepts such as entrepreneurship, marketing, and professional finances, while cultivating fundamental industry skill sets, including leadership, adaptability, and risk analysis.

Computer Science:

Computer Science will equip you with the skills required to thrive in a digital world, regardless of the industry you work in. These skills will be essential to your long-term success. In addition to this it teaches logical and formulaic thinking, creativity, and reliance, not as opposing trails, but as sympathetic to one another.

Drama:

Drama seeks to build your confidence through the physical enactments of empathy, teamwork, and improvisation. It enhances communication, creativity, and performative skills which are essential for a confident persona in a forward-facing workplace.

Design and Technologies:

Design and Technology bridges the expanse between creativity and practicality; it will enable you to understand the significance and beauty of ergonomics and structural integrity. It cultivates problem-solving and project management skills, as well as an understanding of the process of production for everyday items and seeing the beauty of the mundane.

Geography:

Geography has the ability to connect you with the world beyond your window and gain an appreciation for the interconnectivity of our natural environment and human civilisation. It will develop analytical skills and an understanding of how human and natural processes interact with one another to encourage a vision of responsible global citizenship.

History:

History will give you an understanding of how events in our past have impacted and influenced our present and futures. It will hone critical thinking and your ability to evaluate multiple perspectives to draw reasoned and informative conclusions to impact future decisions.

Modern Foreign Languages:

Modern Foreign Languages will open doors to you that you would not have previously considered, providing you with enhanced communication abilities and confidence in communicating with others. It provides a grounding in problem-solving skills and dynamic adaptability when faced with new and unfamiliar situations.

Music:

Music develops your ability to apply self-discipline and structured creativity through the use of a series of algorithmic patterns and constructions. It promotes cognitive skills such as specific memory recollection and manual dexterity.

Physical Education:

Physical Education demonstrates the importance and, vitally, the significance of teamwork and leadership to achieve a common goal. It supports you with negotiation and ambitious target setting within the confines of one's own areas of talent and expertise.

Religious Education:

Religious Education gives you the insight and emotional maturity to see the world from alternative perspectives, which are often foreign, sometimes more literally than figuratively. It enables you to explore diverse beliefs and values while fostering understanding and respect for others.

Action checklist

- [x] Take 30 minutes to engage in "blue-sky thinking" about your subject's curriculum. Ask yourself: "What are the most essential, most valuable, and most future-relevant things I want my students to learn in this subject?" Jot down your ideas and don't censor yourself: think big and bold!
Think: unbound curriculum vision.

- [x] Building from the previous chapter, revisit your department's "subject purpose statement". Review it in light of your "blue-sky thinking". Refine and strengthen the statement to truly capture the essence and long-term value of your subject, beyond exams and curriculum constraints. Share this refined statement with your students, discuss it, and invite their feedback.
Think: articulating enduring subject value.

- [x] At the end of a week, take a few minutes to reflect on your lessons. Ask yourself: "In this week's lessons, did I effectively communicate the purpose and value of my subject?" Identify one thing you could do next week to strengthen the "purpose connection" for your students.
Think: weekly purpose-driven practice.

11 | Mapping your careers curriculum: Identifying strengths and gaps

Summary points

Understanding the Current Curriculum Landscape

Guidance on conducting a baseline audit to help identify existing efforts in the area of careers education in order to analyse whether teacher and student expectations align with the broader landscape of careers.

Collecting and Organising Department Careers Delivery

Develop different approaches to surveys, interviews as well as formal and informal meetings to gain valuable insights into how career skills and job awareness are embedded into the curriculum.

Building a Lasting and Purposeful Careers Framework

Encoding a curriculum map to highlight impactful moments of careers learning, highlighting opportunities for industry links and engagement.

Knowing the current state of play among staff is a crucial starting point for establishing any school-wide programme, whether it is careers-related or not. The purpose of this is not to catch people out or highlight their gaps. Instead, it is about discovering what teachers and students expect from a careers programme. It also involves learning about their daily practice in relation to careers.

It has been mentioned before, but it is worth reiterating the point: teachers work hard. They also underestimate the impact that they have in terms of the lessons they are actually teaching. The point of a baseline audit is to find out what else is happening in classrooms, in subjects, in a student's day, which contribute to a wider careers programme.

Learning point

Much like when playing darts, going in blind is unlikely to produce a satisfactory outcome. Be prepared, in that you know what you want to discover, or not, as you work through. Are you after explicit examples of career, or possibly more aptly, job, information in relation to the curriculum? Are you after examples of skills being delivered through lesson themes? Are you after examples of opportunities or activities that students have the opportunity to gain insight into the world beyond their education? The list can be quite extensive once you get going; some sensible starting points would be:

For teachers:

- What careers does your subject prepare students for?
    - How does it do this?
    - How are students made aware of this?
    - Is this written into the curriculum/lesson plans?
- What transferable skills does your subject provide students with?
    - How does it do this?
    - How are students made aware of this?
    - Is this written into the curriculum/lesson plans?
    - Outside of lesson time, does your subject provide opportunities for students to explore careers related to it? Examples include, but are not limited to:
        - External speakers
        - Curriculum contributions
        - Trips and visits
        - Workshops and off-timetable activities
        - Extracurricular activities and clubs

For students:

- Which jobs/careers would you most associate with each subject?
    - Why have you chosen this?
    - What have you learnt in this subject that would support you with this?
    - How would you go about becoming qualified to do this job/career?

11| Mapping Your Careers Curriculum: Identifying Strengths and Gaps

> - How often, would you say, is future careers or application to the real world referenced in a lesson?
> - How is information about which jobs/careers are available to go into nationally and locally communicated with you?
>
> One thing to make clear with all contributors is that it is not about trying to catch anyone out; there is no shame in answering "no", and no expectations to answer "yes". It is about gaining an honest and accurate picture of how the land lies at this point in time.

While this activity is very much a stand-alone one, with little obvious options for development, it is essential. Without a systematic approach to gathering and recording information, careers programmes will continue in a disjointed and non-cohesive manner and eventually break down. There is no reason to stop with staff and students: consider how core data is obtained from partner businesses, parents, governors, or visiting VIPs. How is it gathered, recorded, and actioned?

Evidently, having a careers integration programme that goes beyond the curriculum and into the heart of a school is incredibly powerful. But it is never as straightforward as simply asking people a question and getting an answer; it will take time and needs consistency of its interpretation by all parties.

When it comes to completing a physical audit, the process is very similar to that of any auditing tool. Setting a series of parameters and marking how frequently and where these parameters are met. The question then comes down to: "What are your parameters?"

Simple job vs skills audit

Very similar to the primary example provided earlier in this book, at a secondary level this can be extended to include information on the next stage or transition options to help build the visibility of pathways into industry for students. It will also enable teaching staff to be more fluent in their discussions of the optional and progression routes available to students.

The principle behind it is very simple: convert key elements of a careers programme into a simplified code. This coding is then applied to any planning or strategic documentation whenever the opportunity to express it arises. The coding is entirely down to your programme and can be as simple or complex as needed.

Skills (single letter)

Allocate to each skills category a code: this can be a generic set of skills, a chosen framework's set of skills or your own developed framework's skills focus; it is up to you. Take the opportunity to provide definitions which relate closely to their academic and development level, make it age appropriate.

- Communication as C
- Problem-Solving as P

Industry (double letter)

A similar coding is then applied for industry. Populating the headings with examples of roles within the industry not only helps in building teachers' knowledge base but also provides examples which are not necessarily the most obvious. Sticking to industry sectors as opposed to jobs enables this category to be applicable over multiple years; jobs change, industries are consistent.

- Healthcare as He
- Construction as Co

Transition/progression (triple letter)

To follow the theme of encoding, different transition routes gain a different code. Add to this examples of types of course which can be taken to progress within it. You may want to leave gaps where each subject can add into it subjects/courses which relate to their subjects.

- Academic as Aca
- Vocational as Voca
- Apprenticeship/training as App

11| Mapping Your Careers Curriculum: Identifying Strengths and Gaps

Careers framework excerpt:

Category	Subcategory	Key Stage	Coding
Reference to "skill"	Communication: *taking turns speaking, listening to others, asking questions, and explaining thoughts.*	3	3S.C
Reference to "skill"	Communication: *working in teams, sharing ideas, asking questions, listening carefully, and presenting information clearly.*	4	4S.C
Reference to "skill"	Problem-Solving: *exploring ideas, trying different solutions, asking for help, and learning through play.*	3	3S.P
Reference to "skill"	Problem-Solving: *working in teams, brainstorming ideas, testing solutions, and learning from mistakes.*	4	4S.P
...	...	...	...
Reference to "job"	Healthcare: *e.g. Pharmacist, Physiotherapist, Optician*	3	3J.He
Reference to "job"	Healthcare: *e.g. Neurologist, Radiotherapist*	4	4J.He
Reference to "job"	Construction: *e.g. Architect. Civil Engineer, Surveyor*	3	3J.Co
Reference to "job"	Construction: *e.g. Site Manager, Health and Safety Official*	4	4J.Co
...	...	...	...
Reference to "transition"	Academic: *A Levels, Degrees, Masters etc.* Courses:	4	4T.Aca
Reference to "transition"	Vocational: *Btecs, T Levels, NVQs* Courses:	4	4T.Voc
Reference to "transition"	Apprenticeship/Training: Courses:	4	4T.App

Depending on the needs of your school, you may or may not need all three categories (Job, Skill, and Transition). It may very well be more suitable to only use one or two of these and keep it stripped back to only the points which you deem the most impactful on students. Ultimately though, it comes down to time, it is better to do less, but make it meaningful than to dilute down a larger array of spec points simply for size's sake.

Once created, this becomes the ultimate careers reference document. It can be used to annotate any other piece of work being used by staff when preparing lessons or activities for students. Be it a lesson observation pro forma, strategic long-term plans, or even in the slide notes of a presentation, it can be developed to include and emphasise a deeper careers-related learning in practically anything.

Forces

Understanding of forces, their effects on motion, and their relevance in everyday life. Students will learn to identify, measure, and analyse forces, applying Newton's Laws of Motion to explain and predict the behaviour of objects.

No.	Title	Spec.	Obj.	Req.
...	...	...	...	...
4	Friction	- Explain the concept of friction and its effects on motion. - Describe factors that affect friction. - Explain air resistance as a type of frictional force. - Investigate how surface area and speed affect air resistance using simple experiments. 3S.P - Discuss the applications of friction and air resistance in everyday life. 3J.Co 3J.Au	- Describe friction as a force that opposes motion. - Explain how friction and air resistance affect motion. 3S.A - Investigate factors affecting frictional forces.	- Trolly and masses - Paper and masses

11| Mapping Your Careers Curriculum: Identifying Strengths and Gaps

No.	Title	Spec.	Obj.	Req.
5	Newton's First Law	- State and explain Newton's First Law of Motion. - Describe examples of inertia in everyday life. - Explain how inertia affects the motion of objects. 3J.Au - Relate inertia to mass.	- Understand Newton's First Law of Motion. - Explain how mass affects inertia. - Describe examples of inertia. 3J.Co	-Trolleys
6	Newton's Third Law	- State and explain Newton's Third Law of Motion. - Identify action-reaction pairs in various scenarios. - Explain how Newton's Third Law applies to everyday situations. 3S.A - Distinguish between action-reaction pairs and balanced forces.	- Understand Newton's Third Law of Motion. - Identify action-reaction force pairs. - Apply Newton's Third Law to explain phenomena. 3J.Co	- Spring recoil car 3S.P - Skateboard

3S.P - Skill - Problem-Solving 3J.Co - Job - Construction Industry
3S.A - Skill - Analysis 3J.Au - Job - Automotive Industry

It doesn't mean that every single minute of every single day needs to be referencing this document. It doesn't even need to be actioned in lessons every time it appears in planning. It is about ensuring that it remains at the forefront of everyone's minds when they are preparing to engage with a student. Having codes, such as these, scattered across documentation makes it difficult to hide from. It sparks conversation with new staff who see it for the first time, especially when it keeps cropping up; it's mysterious and a bit cheeky. Little things like this also help with the induction process. It doesn't need a huge amount of dedicated off-timetable or CPD time to explain the subtleties of an integrated careers system, just a reference document and an explanation of how to use it. From there it is down to the teacher to take it in whichever direction they see fit.

This approach can be referred to to produce department careers learning profiles. As with most things, it can be as detailed and comprehensive as it needs to be, from a single-page profile to a detailed booklet. Rather than annotating the scheme of learning with the chosen framework or auditing points, instead, annotate around the key points or areas of the framework with the department's self assessment against it.

Using the same sample audit framework as above and the Science department as the example, it can produce a document that, in one place, can summarise the department's contribution to a school-wide career programme. Not only as a "poster" of information to share with relevant parties, but will also serve as a tool for staff to support with the articulation of the wider-reaching impacts of their curriculum.

Category	Subcategory	Key Stage	Subject Connection	Specific Reference
Reference to "Job"	Healthcare: e.g. Pharmacist, Physiotherapist, Optician	3	Biology: Students learn how the body works, enabling them to understand health and medication. Chemistry: Students explore basic chemical interactions, vital for understanding how medicines work.	- Human body systems - Simple chemical reactions
	Healthcare: e.g. Neurologist, Radiotherapist	4	Biology: Students delve into the complexities of the nervous system and how diseases affect it. Physics: Students understand how radiation interacts with the body, crucial for safe and effective treatments.	- Nervous system - Ionising radiation
	Construction: e.g. Architect, Civil Engineer, Surveyor	3	Physics: Students investigate forces and material properties, learning how structures stay standing.	- Forces and motion - Properties of materials
	Construction: e.g. Site Manager, Health and Safety Official	4	Physics: Students apply their knowledge of mechanics to ensure structural safety. Chemistry: Students understand the properties of materials and potential hazards.	- Materials and properties - Chemical hazards

11| Mapping Your Careers Curriculum: Identifying Strengths and Gaps

Category	Subcategory	Key Stage	Subject Connection	Specific Reference
...	...	...	...	...
Reference to "skill"	Communication: *taking turns speaking, listening to others, asking questions, and explaining thoughts.*	3	Science encourages students to articulate their observations and ideas, fostering clear communication during experiments and discussions.	- Application of the scientific method in all practical investigations
	Communication *working in teams, sharing ideas, asking questions, listening carefully, and presenting information clearly.*	4	Through group projects and presentations, students learn to convey complex scientific information effectively, building teamwork and presentation skills.	- Core practical investigations where there are simultaneous actions which require clear communication and synchronisation
	Problem-Solving: *exploring ideas, trying different solutions, asking for help, and learning through play.*	3	The scientific method promotes critical thinking and problem-solving skills through planning, conducting, and evaluating investigations.	- Survival on a desert island activity in a purification topic
	Problem-Solving: *working in teams, brainstorming ideas, testing solutions, and learning from mistakes.*	4	Students develop advanced problem-solving skills by analysing complex data, refining procedures, and learning from experimental errors.	- Consistent approach to core practical elements with a blank state starting approach
...	...	...	...	...
Reference to "transition"	Academic *A Levels, Degrees, Masters etc.*		*A level*: Biology, Chemistry, Physics, Environmental Science *Undergrad Degree*: Engineering (Civil, Mechanical, Electrical, Chemical), Biochemistry, Biological Sciences	
	Vocational *Btecs, T Levels, NVQs*		*Btec*: Applied Science, Health and Social Care, Engineering *T Level*: Health, Engineering and Manufacturing *NVQ*: Lab Technician, Environmental Conservation	
	Apprenticeship/Training		*Apprenticeship*: Healthcare Assistant, Pharmacy Technician, Nuclear Engineer, Water Treatment Technician	

> **Author's note**
>
> This example is deliberately generic to demonstrate the universality of its application to any subject in any school. As with any documentation that is created within a school, the more specific to the school, the better; it gives it a real purpose that isn't simply ticking a box which was dictated by the Careers Leader or Leadership Team.

However, in the recording of everyone's contribution to the overall delivery, the most important thing, by a country mile, is that everyone is involved in its creation and delivery. Keeping these documents live and reviewed semi-regularly is important. As teachers move on, curriculums change and school development plans, well, develop. Documents like this can very quickly fall to the wayside and become lost and irrelevant, relics of an initiative that never took off.

Once they have been created, be creative in their usage. Producing posters to contribute to classroom displays is a great way to bring all subjects together. You can also compile these into a single booklet that can be published on the website or used during open and options evenings. Even better, using these materials directly with students and inviting their contributions for future editions creates a powerful tool for engagement and longevity.

> **STAFF SUPPORT RESOURCE**
>
> There are several methods of data gathering, each with its benefits and limitations. It is important to use the ones which best suit your needs, abilities, and access.
>
> ### Small group interviews and discussions
>
> This method promotes a more natural response among those who are present. Due to the smaller size, participants are often more confident to contribute their own opinions in addition to the factual responses regarding the current practice.
>
> It is, however, much harder to record the information collected as conversations can often be spoken faster than they are recorded and can become intangible when taken out of context. In addition to this, it is also a rather lengthy process with multiple meetings needing to take place among staff and students in order to build a full and representative picture. Consider using this method to augment larger data collection and delve further into a particular point of interest which might arise.

Anonymous digital or paper surveys

This method is likely to gain honest answers from participants; it will provide opinions and feedback which is highly personal to those who answer it. Depending on how it is phrased and distributed, it can provide very quantifiable data which will aid in the analysis and summarisation.

Due to its nature, however, it needs to be completed in relative isolation. This means that there will not always be the opportunity to clarify understanding or probe further into answers about which it would be beneficial to know more. Equally, it can be difficult to standardise the quality/quantity of answers given and even the number of responses if it coincides with particular pinch points in the year.

Consider using this method if obtaining face-to-face time is difficult to obtain or is only available for short periods of time. For it to be most effective, it will need a clear briefing and a simple format with direct and prescriptive expectation of response.

Middle leader meetings/discussions

These meetings tend to happen more frequently than whole staff meetings. This increases the likelihood of finding a time that is suitable and falls at the most convenient point in the year. They also provide an opportunity to bring together all the curriculum leaders. These leaders have oversight and decision-making authority over the entire school's curriculum. Speaking to staff in this setting allows you to gather each department's big picture when it comes to careers learning built into their schemes of work.

While this approach is very useful for gaining a broad-strokes collection of information. It is less successful at collecting the more nuanced aspects of individual teacher and classroom experiences that occur when teachers put their own stamps on lessons and lesson planning. It also very much relies on trust that the information that is being given and received is being gathered and disseminated throughout teams.

If time is at a premium then this will enable rapid information gathering and distribution with the potential for regular follow ups and feedback.

Individual departmental meetings

The benefit of working with whole departments or faculties for a dedicated period of time is that there is the opportunity to gain highly personal and specific insights into the ethos and methodology of a department. It is a chance to work with staff to not only audit their careers learning approach but also support and offer guidance, particularly in how they can begin to further integrate it into their daily practice and their mid- and long-term plans.

This process takes time; there are not many opportunities for departments to come together and not have a time-pressing agenda that must be dealt with. This could take months to gather in total. The temptation will be to combine departments together. Careful now, while this would reduce the number of meetings which would need to occur, it will also dilute the information and quality of conversation which can be generated.

These meetings are a fantastic way to further delve deeper into a subject and discover what makes it pop; however it can take months to fully work through the entire school.

Whole staff meetings/CPD

Having the dedicated time to work with all staff is a real luxury, especially if careers education isn't widely prevalent within the school, or if it is being developed properly for the first time. It will raise the profile of the work being completed and the significance it plays, alongside the standard curriculum, in a student's education. In addition to this, it will enable the clear communication of the rationale and expectations of completing a whole-school audit of a student's careers education while in school.

Bringing everyone together is tough. Yes, there are probably a lot of times throughout the year when this is possible and there will almost certainly be frequent occasions when 15 minutes can be allocated here and there. However, in order for this to be effective and meaningful, you will need to barter for a bit more time. In order to introduce and allow significant time to explore and summarise, you should be looking at periods closer to one-and-a-half to two hours.

Action checklist

☑ Dedicate a department meeting to a baseline curriculum audit at the secondary level. Ask teachers to review one Key Stage 3 or Key Stage 4 scheme of work and identify existing career links and skill development opportunities relevant to secondary students. The aim is to get a "snapshot" of current provision, not a comprehensive overhaul.

Think: realistic baseline assessment, secondary focus.

11| Mapping Your Careers Curriculum: Identifying Strengths and Gaps

- ☑ Choose one subject area at secondary level and conduct a more detailed audit using the "Careers Framework excerpt". Adapt the categories (Job, Skill, Transition) to best fit your subject and school context. The goal is to trial using a framework to map careers links more systematically within a secondary subject.

  Think: framework familiarisation – secondary subject focus, not perfection.

- ☑ Discuss: Is audit information usable for secondary teachers? Does it highlight any gaps or strengths in current careers provision for secondary students? What are one or two realistic "next steps" your department/school could take to build on this baseline at the secondary level?

  Think: action-oriented review and planning.

12 | Working with parents: A partnership for career success

Summary points

Parents: The Untapped Careers for Educators

Recognise and leverage the existing career influence parents have; they are a student's first and often most influential careers educators, shaping values and aspirations from day one.

"Hijack" Parental Touchpoints

Don't create brand new events; efficiency is key. Strategically "hijack" existing school events where parents are already engaged and present, like parents' evenings and open days, to subtly and organically weave in key careers messages and opportunities for involvement, maximising your reach without extra effort

Consistent Drip-Feed, Not a Firehose

For effective parental engagement, remember that consistency trumps intensity. Focus on a regular, manageable drip-feed of careers communication and opportunities throughout the year, rather than overwhelming parents with a firehose of information all at once.

"It takes a village to raise a child" or so the proverb goes. There is a reason why proverbs such as this stick around in our collective consciousness. It's true. It cannot be the sole responsibility of parents to instil the values of becoming conscious citizens. Equally, it cannot be the sole responsibility of teachers and schools to prepare students for the world of work and find their passions in it. It is a team effort; it has to be so. Teachers and parents must be a combined unit. Lord help the students whose parents are teachers; those poor souls don't stand a chance. Working with parents is more than just helpful; it is vital to helping students reach their full potential.

As all in education will be acutely aware, there is a wide level and degree of engagement from their parental cohorts. This is an incredibly tricky minefield to navigate and is laden with obstacles which can be varied and incredibly difficult to navigate. But when it is done right, the impact it can have on young people is transformative. When they have the knowledge that they have support and guidance from all areas of their lives they are far more likely to take risks knowing they are in an environment which will catch them.

As is the theme of this book, doing extra is not always worth extra. Making better use of what already exists and is in place is often the most effective use of time and resources. For example, there are many touchpoints in a student's trip through education where parents are requested to be directly involved: parents' evenings, open events, information evenings, awards evenings, to name but a few. Hijacking these opportunities to sow the seeds of careers education is a great way of raising awareness in a natural and organic way. Unlike other subjects, careers learning can be introduced in pretty much any situation without it seeming like it has been shoehorned in. It straddles across the academic as well as the pastoral sides of education while still maintaining a laser focus on the future.

Learning point

Every September, parents are invited to an information evening whereby they receive what is effectively an elongated assembly from the leadership and pastoral team. They are introduced to the tutor team and given all of the required contact information that they require and the various lines of communication. Along with this, they receive the mandatory lectures about attendance, uniform, behaviour, and equipment expectations.

These are obviously very important and genuinely do need to be restated. But by the time students have been in a school a number of years it can become quite repetitive. This isn't to say that introducing a careers element to it is going to save the day or change the dynamic of the whole affair. What it does do, however, is highlight and bring to mind that schools are here to prepare young people for the world of work and transition into adulthood. Using repeat engagements keeps this message clear and consistent, while at the same time serving to remind everyone that they play a vital and unique role in a student's education.

All it takes is 5 minutes, ideally a little longer, but if 5 minutes is what you can get, then 5 minutes is all it needs. Make them count.

> Much in the same way that heads of year will have their own vision for each year, each year needs a clear and concise careers vision to frame the next 12 months of school. These meetings are an ideal opportunity to introduce the narrative for that cohort of students' engagement and the overall desired outcomes. Theming each year group is key to creating the chronological story that will be told throughout the entirety of school, while helping to reduce annual repetition.
>
> Start with transition, entry, and raising awareness in Year 7 bringing in the excitement of change and new beginnings, while at the same time hinting at a greater purpose at play. The phrase "you can't be what you can't see" epitomises this; this year is all about exploring new possibilities and experiencing new opportunities.
>
> As students move through the year groups themes can develop and reflect on their journey to that point, such as the choosing of GCSE options in Year 9 and the concept of following interests and looking at future pathways. Year 10 is the year of looking outward for the first time, and taking charge of their futures, normally centralised around the starting of GCSEs and the benefits brought by well-researched work experience placements.

These are by no means prescriptive; they will always depend on the school's priorities and must be delivered alongside the core messages being delivered such that they complement, not compete with, the evening's message. Weaving the message that careers education is everywhere, all the time, into as many parental events as possible will begin to take the narrative out of the classroom and into the homes of students. Going further still there is the chance to take full advantage that a captive audience provides. The platform to raise awareness of the need for volunteers and participants, and that, while they might not feel like they have much to offer, engagement is everything.

A word of warning: know when to stop. Trying to share everything that is happening and every way in which they can get involved will just as likely alienate as it will rally. Set a solid foundation of carefully placed bricks rather than dumping them all in a pile at once; it will be sturdier, last longer, and ultimately just look better.

STAFF SUPPORT RESOURCE

Over the course of a year, there will be several touchpoints, each of these can be used to encourage parents to engage in different facets of a programme. Helping ensure that it reaches out of the school and into students' lives as a whole.

Awards evenings

These probably aren't the best opportunities to be trying to peddle your wares as a careers leader to parents. This is a moment of celebration of students' contributions to school, let's keep it that way. That's not to say that there isn't the opportunity to have a bit of an influence on it and be a little bit sneaky in slipping it in, it just takes a bit of lateral thinking.

Every good awards evening starts with a welcome message. The theme of this message tends to be based around the celebration of the forthcoming students' success. The overarching reason as to why they are worthy and deserving of celebration. Of course this is important, but it can be a little perfunctory. Make use of a Careers Leader's network to invite guest speakers to instead address students and parents on the importance of looking to the future and inspiring future success. They don't need to be expensive after-dinner speakers; often the best are the people who have been involved in the careers programme and know the context of the school. They can bridge the gap between education and the world and celebrate the impact of lifelong learning.

Open events

Open events for prospective students and families give schools the opportunity to showcase their facilities and passionate staff. They frequently focus on the academic offer through the curriculum or the extracurricular opportunities that are made available to students. So why not the intra-curricular? Use these moments to showcase the importance of an interwoven career programme that will run throughout their school experience.

- Make it part of each subject department's display/presentations.
- Celebrate the destinations of students who have left, both recent and legacy, in terms of colleges and sixth forms as well as professions.
- Invite some of your most engaged community partners to speak about their involvement.

- Treat it like a department with the same presence as a subject would have, with resources and activities.
- Bring in your industry partners to stand with you side by side, put forward a united front.

Introducing this to parents and students from before they start will demystify and break down the misconceptions which so often come up. Especially when careers education is brought up with those of younger students. It turns the thought process from "that's not for us yet, it's a long way off" to "this is part of the process of moving through education". Small changes to mindsets like this begin to smooth out the path ahead.

Newsletters

This might seem obvious, and to be honest, it probably is. However, a well-crafted careers newsletter that is shared with parents on a regular basis, be it weekly, monthly, termly, can serve multiple purposes. It can celebrate the events and opportunities that students have experienced or taken part in, highlighting the extra work that is taking place within the school. It can showcase opportunities that are available within the community for students and their families to participate in which extend on the learning taking place in school. It can focus in on a particular element of the careers programme, or framework, explaining its importance in life and application within the curriculum, as well as suggesting ways in which this learning and application might be continued at home through discussions and activities.

Drop-in morning/afternoons

This comes in two flavours, the first of which is providing drop-in support hubs for parents. These may take the forms/theme of whatever is current or relevant at the time, ranging from supporting Work Experience placements to Application and CV writing workshops to be able to better support their children at home. Engagement is always going to be varied; it will take time to build the reputation of providing meaningful meetings. This can be fast-tracked by inviting guest speakers such as Careers Hubs, or Parent Teacher Associations (PTAs) to host keynote spots, maximising the benefit with the need for minimal meetings.

The sports halls are often rented out to local clubs; who says the same can't be done with conference rooms? Granted, these are not always the norm, especially if they are arranged with a careers-specific focus. But, making use of school facilities to provide hubs of support or engagement for the community has the potential

> to open dialogues and connections that would otherwise go unexplored. Inviting the local Chamber of Commerce, or hosting your MP for round table meetings, might seem like a far cry from a careers programme. But inviting people like this to make use of school spaces provides the perfect opportunity to showcase the work you are doing, sharing the opportunities for engagement with students first-hand. Nothing sells like experience.

Action checklist

- ☑ At your next parents' or information evening, identify one opportunity to subtly weave in a careers message. This could be a brief mention in a presentation, a careers-focused question for tutors to discuss with parents, or a handout signposting to careers resources for families.
  Think: strategic, low-lift integration.

- ☑ For your next school open event, ensure careers education has a visible presence. This could include a dedicated careers display, showcasing student destinations, inviting community partners to participate, or incorporating careers information into subject department presentations.
  Think: making careers unmissable.

- ☑ Commit to creating a regular careers newsletter for parents (start with termly if that feels manageable). For your first edition, focus on celebrating recent careers activities at school, highlighting community opportunities for families, or explaining one key aspect of your school's careers programme. Keep it concise, engaging, and action-oriented for parents.
  Think: consistent home-school careers communication.

PART III

Putting frameworks into action

> The intentions of a tool are what it does. A hammer intends to strike, a vice intends to hold fast, a lever intends to lift. They are what it is made for.
>
> Philip Pullman, *The Amber Spyglass*

Summary points

Choose the Right Framework
Select a curriculum framework that aligns with your school's ethos and goals; whether static, progressive, or a custom-built model. Ensure it supports students' long-term career readiness development.

Ensure Staff and Student Engagement
Involve all stakeholders, including teachers, students and leadership, in the design and implementation of your chosen careers education integration framework to create a lasting impact and prevent it from becoming another superficial exercise.

Plan for Long-Term Sustainability
Build a system that is adaptable, easy to integrate, and forward-thinking, ensuring consistency throughout leadership changes and remaining relevant to students' future career pathways.

Having worked with staff to support their delivery of a curriculum, you will have started to build a provision. One that is more than the pursuit of knowledge; that is truly inclusive and meaningful to students. It is now time to think about how this will be recorded and physically implemented across the school. There are plenty of models out there which will provide you with frameworks and progressive levels of objectives or benchmarks. Quite honestly, it is something of a minefield, just less dangerous. Deciding on the right one for you is down to personal preference. Which one speaks to you on a personal and professional level? What is right for your school at this point in time and where do you want to be in the next few years?

Regardless of the framework that is settled upon, there is a commonality between all of them: education does a pretty good job of the academic side of things. It has been doing its thing for a very long time now. Careers frameworks therefore tend to focus on everything else. Everything that can, does, or should happen in a school other than academic prowess. Broadly speaking, they can be broken down into two overarching categories: Static and Progressive.

Static

These frameworks are, as their name implies, fixed regardless of age, subject, or setting. They are often quite generic in their approach, highlighting key areas of learning or skill criteria which enable them to be broadly applied across school settings. These types of frameworks lend themselves to schools which standardise their lesson structures and teaching and learning initiatives across the whole school.

They often include single-word identifiers with broad descriptors which enable them to be widely adopted into a number of different contexts and subjects. For this reason, they can be interpreted and worked into most school systems regardless of their overarching ethos or development plans. Little tweaks here or minor adjustments and rephrases there will pretty much guarantee that it will slide right in.

In terms of implementation, staff and department leads can, with relative ease, map these models onto existing schemes of work. Done by highlighting onto progression maps or signposting in lessons where certain aspects of the framework are relevant. This has the advantage that it can be broadly applied across many subjects simultaneously with relative ease, it simply requires the time taken to sit down with a scheme of work and framework descriptors (and a fair few coloured pens or highlighters). Full school integration can be achieved in a couple of hours taking up one, or maybe two, staff training sessions to introduce and apply it.

It is, however, let down by its intrinsic nature to be broad and simple. It requires students to be literate in its meaning, and often nuanced language, to fully understand its purpose in order to link it to the curriculum and the world outside of education. It also runs the risk of quickly becoming a tick-box exercise for members of staff, particularly if it is rushed into with little to no context. It risks becoming stagnant for students who do not see it progressing as they do.

Teamwork, for example, could be, and often is, one of the descriptive points. Teamwork in earlier years will mean something very different to students entering their GCSEs. After seeing, or hearing, the word "teamwork" unchanging in meaning for five consecutive years in a series of increasingly complex scenarios, it can become juvenile. Perceived as a more immature skill to which was important when they joined the school, but less so as they leave.

Static frameworks do, however, allow for the systemic auditing of effectiveness, in particular in terms of inter-institutional comparisons and standardisation if the same frameworks are in place in multiple schools.

> **What's out there? Static frameworks**
>
> There are numerous static frameworks out there to incorporate into your setting. They tend to have a specific focus or theme, which can be an excellent way to shine light on a particular part of your curriculum or school life. Below are several frameworks of interest which can be broadly categorised into the static model.

Putting Frameworks into Action

The Education 4.0 Taxonomy proposed by the World Economic Forum

Developed by the World Economic Forum and published in their 2023 white paper, this framework sets out the proposed future needs of the employment sector, taking into account lifelong learning. It has two broad areas of application: the Framework and the Taxonomy of Skills.

The Framework addresses the overarching need for the development of future-ready skills in childhood education and provides a common foundation for all parties to work from. With an emphasis placed on building and developing uniquely human attributes. This is split into two key areas: Content and Experiences. Content referring to the mechanisms which enable core skill application and experience referring to pedagogical approach to delivering these.

The Taxonomy of Skills sets out the aptitudes that are crucial to a future-ready generation, built into a three-tier hierarchy which categorises them into higher order thinking. These skills can be used in a mix and match fashion when set against student learning or cognitive application, clearly highlighting the importance of interdisciplinary approach to lifelong learning.

Teaching for Creativity developed by Winchester and Halterworth Creativity Collaborative

Teaching for Creativity sets out to provide a learning cycle to foster creativity as a core quality to build into every aspect of a student's educational journey. Developed in conjunction with primary education, tried and tested with students within the classroom. It provides a tool for staff to be used to develop a curriculum that is inclusive and founded in inspiring a creative teaching and learning approach to education.

It is centred around the Teaching for Creativity Planning Tool, which becomes a mantra like approach to curriculum design and lesson planning and sits deeply inside the curriculum, applied to all areas of learning. Due to its specific nature, time and buy-in from staff is essential as it requires a change in approach from the ground up. However, once implemented it provides an agency for creativity and emphasises creativity as a lifelong learning tool.

Creative habits (of mind) developed by Centre for Real-World Learning

Creative habits set out to provide a tool to support teachers and learners in fostering and developing creativity in their practice. They have identified the five creative habits as: Imaginative, Inquisitive, Collaborative, Disciplined, and Persistent.

> The five habits are universally applicable to all key stages, setting a clear language of creativity that can be applied to all contexts of education. It also sees the potential in its incorporation into professional life as a framework adopted by industry sectors in the same manner.
>
> **The Diamond Model as part of Social Pedagogy by ThemPra Social Pedagogy Community Interest Company**
>
> While not specifically a model for careers education, The Diamond Model is designed to put learners at its centre and is built around the fact that every human is unique and multifaceted in ways which are waiting to be realised. Their model is therefore wholly encompassing of the individual. It seeks to provide a positive learning and development experience, focusing on: well-being and happiness, empowerment, relationships, and potentially the most important, holistic learning.
>
> This framework has been included as an example of what is out there for the simple fact that through its integration it will support all learners in finding meaning and purpose in education and life. Therefore, intended or not, career.

Progressive

A progressive framework is one that is structured to build and develop with the students as they progress through their educational journeys. They tend to be based around several overarching points, themes, or areas of learning. Incorporating the concept of a laddered or incremental stepped approach to learning. For this reason, they are closely aligned to how students naturally learn. Through the setting of solid foundations and gradually building up to a visible, achievable and tangible goal at the end. This dynamic approach means that they can be used by staff independently and do not require the explicit signposting or overt identification systematically put in places across the school. They mirror the spiralled curriculum which is present in many schools, for these reasons.

Implementing these frameworks into the existing curriculum will often require more than a single meeting or training session. They are much more reliant on a progressive or spiralled curriculum for them to build themselves into. For this reason and in order for them to be deeply set in and have meaningful impact on students, the staff delivering it must also be the ones who are given the time to explore it and map it into their existing curriculums. In doing so it will enable it to blend organically into the teaching of the subject, rather than a jarring bolt on to it.

Putting Frameworks into Action

Progressive frameworks, much like their curriculum counterparts, take time to demonstrate their worth. They aren't, they can't be, quick wins or fixes that will set off fireworks in the first term of implementation. For them to become embedded and start taking on a real effect will take a couple of years at the least. Certainly not for the faint-hearted, but if given the opportunity to grow, will become more than just a bolted on programme, but part of the heart of a school.

What's out there? Progressive frameworks

There are numerous progressive frameworks out there to incorporate into your setting. They tend to build over time across several key categories or skills which are tailored to the students' educational journey. Below are several frameworks of interest which can be broadly categorised into the model.

The eight essential skills produced by the Skills Builder Partnership

Also referred to as the Skills Builder Framework, this is one of the most universally used frameworks across education as well as professional industry and outreach. It consists of eight skills essential for the development of a student throughout their educational journey. Each of which is broken down into a sequence of steps that build from introduction to mastery, steps 0 to 15.

Due to its wide-ranging use, particularly in educational outreach, it can be clearly signposted to students and staff and incorporated into wider school life. As with all progressive frameworks, if used in partnership with feeder and destination settings, it provides students with a consistent message and learning journey regardless of the stage of their education. Giving them practical and identifiable achievements throughout all years of their education.

Six learning areas of the Career Development Institute's Career Development Framework for primary schools and secondary schools and colleges

This framework sews a journey through student education from Early Years through to college and sixth form. It is split into six key learning areas: Growth throughout life; Explore possibilities; Manage Career; Create opportunities; Balance life and work; and See the big picture. Within each learning area there contains the laddered journey broken down into actionable points. It provides a holistic checklist which can be applied across all aspects of school life and enables whole school contributions. Throughout it highlights the core skills and attitudes that are at the heart of a meaningful and affirming career.

Due to its holistic overview of education, it is effective at becoming written into the context of whichever school it is applied to. It can be implemented implicitly or explicitly depending on its need and function within the school giving it a high level of adaptability and customisation of delivery.

Meta-skills Progression Framework published by Skills Development Scotland

Set up to tackle the unknown future of jobs that is facing students once they leave education, the Meta-skills Progression Framework seeks to improve the employability of young people as they enter the world of work. It is important to note that this framework, specifically, is not designed to be used by students. It is designed to be used by the teaching staff to evaluate and bring into their daily practice.

As with many frameworks, it is broken down into several main themes. In this case: Self-management, Social Intelligence, and Innovation and then further broken up into four tangible sub categories which are directly applied to student learning. It targets students from the point at which they enter education in the Early Years setting and follows them through to adulthood.

Skills for Life, Learning and Work created by Perth and Kinross Council

The Skills of Life, Learning and Work was created for the educational settings within the Perth and Kinross Council area. It highlights the importance of the acquisition, articulation, and development of life long skills. It identifies that to list and quantify all skills would be impractical, that the relevance and significance of particular skills will be curriculum-, subject-, and even teacher-dependent.

While this framework isn't explicitly progressive, meaning it doesn't advance step-by-step with students as they move through their education, it does focus on a universal application of skills. These skills are relevant at all stages and build alongside growing confidence as students become more adept each year.

There is a third option, and it is not for the faint-hearted: to create a custom-built framework that fits to the mould of your school, regardless of phase or cohorts. This can often be seen as a huge amount of work that needs deep-setting in research and evidence, taking years to compile and analyse . However, the truth of it is that the only thing it must be, is suitable for the students, deliverable by the staff, and consistent with the school's ethos and vision. It is of course important that there is evidence backing it up, but a lot of this is already compiled here for you.

Building your own

Building your own framework is a powerful tool to develop for your school; it is entirely organic and is bespoke to your setting. It has the added advantage that it can be written into the school's ethos and policies in such a way that it no longer is an integration into the curriculum, but rather THE curriculum. It will require the contribution of every member of staff to build; everyone who comes in contact with students, within these settings, must be living and breathing the school ethos. It therefore must have their contribution.

Research is still important. It is completely possible to outline a set of standards that you hold to be true, which you identify as vital for students' career and personal development, but they are highly likely to be biased by your own experience and your own opinions on the matter. Seeking support from school leaders and teaching staff can be hugely beneficial. They will be able to bring their own experience and passions to the table. This too, however, is not without its risks; the more people that are contributing, the more ideas that are fighting for prominence. The more likely the water is to become muddied and lose the initial focus and cohesion.

Understanding future trends from both national and international perspectives will help shape your framework into something bespoke and personal to your environment. At the same time, it ensures the framework remains highly relevant and grounded in evidence. This can involve reviewing LSIP (Local Skills Improvement Plans) reports, looking at World Economic Forum reviews, and keeping up with various Government White Papers released throughout the year. It also includes consulting with local representatives from Chambers of Commerce. There is a lot to disseminate in these documents. Setting a firm foundation in well-documented and researched evidence will build longevity into your framework. Meaning that only minor adjustments need to be made over time to maintain local and national relevance.

Creating a custom fit framework is not without its challenges; it must be a team effort, particularly if it is being developed into an established setting and has an existing ethos which this is to be worked into. Gathering initial impressions from student voice, staff surveys as well as the teaching and learning team will greatly support this process.

Preparation is key; putting together research prior to bringing staff together to act as a skeleton to flesh out will give a central theme to work from and clarify thought processes. It will also act as a point of reference throughout and will be key for bringing discussions and documentation back when deviating and delaying on aspects for too long.

Author's note

Do not act alone.

You will need to gather and distil ideas and opinions in order to make sure it is inclusive and rounded. Make use of your cohort of teachers and school leaders to gather input and critique to guide the structure of your build. Everyone's an expert at something; it might not always be academic, but they will have points of contribution which are not to be missed or wasted.

Start small and build.

Once you have the grains of an idea formed, gradually invite more to contribute and critique. This will ensure a core vision remains at its heart populated through the committee and therefore more likely to stick and stay long term.

Think long term.

Please don't use this to start something that is not sustainable and capable of legacy beyond your input. It needs to be simple and usable by experienced and newbie teachers alike. There is nothing more frustrating for a teacher who is told to restructure their curriculum or teaching style based on the whim of the most current research team. An integrated system like this needs to be universal and timeless.

Aim ten years ahead.

Remember that at its heart, it will only have its intended impact well after students have left your school. This needs to be kept at the forefront of all elements from which it is constructed and formed. Just because it is easily applied doesn't mean it is necessarily the right one to include.

 Learning point

Building a framework is very similar to the process of building a lesson. Start with your key Tier 1 themes that your framework addresses; they should be clear but not overly specific. For argument's sake, let's say **Creativity**, **Integrity**, and **Global Citizen**. It doesn't need to be these three; it doesn't actually need to be three, for that matter. What is important is that these key themes speak to the ethos of your setting and are timeless, in the sense that they are universally accepted as core human values.

From this point it is all about ideas, collecting as many different sub or Tier 2 themes as possible. Tier 2 is all about the actionable points that are happening on the ground level. They are the core strands that will run throughout your framework which will need to become part of the lexicon of staff and students. For this reason they must be recognisable, easily definable and, most importantly, relevant to students' futures outside of education. These need to be founded in the research and applicable to students of all ages. The most effective ones will be specific enough that they can be demonstrated within a lesson, but general enough that they can be applied as effectively to a Year 1 class as to a Year 11 one.

Examples of these include **Teamwork, Public Speaking, Self-Efficacy, Grit, Analytics, Problem-Solving,** and **Critical Thinking**. As before, this is by no means an exhaustive list, nor are these going to be the most relevant to your Tier 1 themes. When determining and selecting these, it is important that there is a clear relationship between the grouping of the Tier 2 themes and the parent Tier 1 theme. While there might be an argument for Teamwork, Critical thinking, and Grit to all fall within the Global Citizen theme, it's not obviously apparent. It would need subsequent explanations to justify and would therefore be relatively ineffective and have limited staying power within a curriculum.

In both the Tier 1 and Tier 2 themes, their descriptors must be clear and actionable in such a way that teachers plan them into lessons and signpost them to students, yet also applicable in a range of situations throughout school. This is where your careful collaboration will be most important. Everyone will have their own views on them, it is about bringing them all together in a usable and age-/ability- specific manner.

 Author's note

Questions to ask yourself:

Development

- Does it reference the school's values/ethos?
- Does it address core employability skills/attributes?
- Is it accessible and achievable for students regardless of ability?
- Can it be demonstrated in and out of the classroom?
- What is your success criteria?
- What is your research and evidence founded on?
- What specific issues/areas do you want to address?

Structure

- Will it be progressive or static?
- Can it be applied to pre- and/or post-key stages?
- Is it simple enough for students to readily access it?
- Is it specific enough so that it can be clearly identified in learning and achievement?
- How many themes will it consist of?
- Will you make use of subthemes?
- How will it be presented on a macro and micro scale?

Roles and responsibilities

- What role will teachers have in its implementation?
- What role will senior leaders have in its launch and evaluation?
- What role will students have in its formation and evaluation?
- What role will support staff have in its integration into the whole school life?
- What role will parents have in supplementary engagement?
- How will you launch it with staff and students?
- Who owns it?
- How will you ensure consistency in the long term?

Ultimately it comes down to the team working on it to ensure that all stakeholders are engaged and brought in from its inception. At no point should it be the sole responsibility of a single person to implement and maintain. It is crucial that staff and students alike all see its intrinsic value and worth, such that it eventually becomes the curriculum and not a bolt on. Be warned, if it is unable to take life beyond a single person, it will die with them and become another relic of a series of unused classroom initiatives. Building a legacy is easier said than done, but a good starting point is once it is up and running, step away from its monitoring and evaluation. Counter-intuitive, but essential. While you are holding the reins, there is no incentive for an operational, or even strategic, investment or ownership from other members of staff. Much like the wild mustang with a heart of gold, you must let it go and allow it to be picked up by other members of staff who can lead it into its next phase of implementation and embedding.

Newly established institutions, however, are in that wonderfully unique position of having no resistance to act against. There is no historical standard to which everything must be set up against. You have the freedom to dictate your own imagined curriculum which can be as you want it; this can be centred around your newly created framework rather than working your framework around your curriculum. There can't be resistance to something that hasn't been changed, this is a time which must be taken advantage of, sew it into everything, into each and every part of all systems and processes in such a way that it just is.

Action checklist

☑ Dedicate time to actively explore at least three of the different careers framework examples mentioned in the chapter. Download information, read summaries, and critically review each framework: What are its strengths? Weaknesses? How well does it align with your school's ethos and students' needs?
Think: informed framework selection

☑ Choose your top two framework contenders. Prepare a brief summary outlining the key features, pros/cons, and potential implementation in your school. Share these summaries with your department or a representative group of staff. Facilitate a structured feedback session: Which framework(s) resonate most? Which seems most usable and impactful in your school context?
Think: collaborative framework choice.

☑ Based on your research and staff feedback, choose one framework to "pilot" in one department, one year group, or a small group of teachers for a term or half-term. Keep the pilot focused and manageable. Provide teachers with clear guidance and support for implementation. At the end of the pilot period: What worked well? What were the challenges? What adjustments are needed for wider implementation?
Think: framework testing in practice.

The journey continues

> Then he waited, marshalling his thoughts and brooding over his still untested powers. For though he was master of the world, he was not quite sure what to do next. But he would think of something.
>
> Arthur C. Clarke, *2001: A Space Odyssey*

First up, thank you. Thank you for taking the time to see my perspective, my approach, let's face it, my philosophy for not just career education, but all education.

At the start of this book, I set out three assumptions from which all else followed. I would like to briefly revisit these:

1. **Teachers work hard!**
   I will restate it if it hasn't yet been made clear. Teachers. Work. Hard. It should be clear through the summaries and resources throughout this book that at no point should there be a burden placed on staff to work any harder than before. Much like an anamorphosis projection (had to Google that one), it is about shifting and realigning the perspective from which things are viewed. The constituent components of education and teaching remain the same. The way in which they are thought about and delivered to students is where the change needs to come from, and let the magic happen.

2. **There are pockets of genius unique to you and your school already.**
   An ideal result of working through this book would be that there is no structural change to anything in your school. It has been there all along, tucked up in isolated corners, slowly working along in its own little way. Teachers are phenomenal people. They are masters of their fields. They have the unique skill set to convey its beauty to young people in such a way as to educate them in all its wonder, while simultaneously preparing them for the big, bad world. It is simply a case of collecting together all of the pieces and sewing them together into a lovely careers-y quilt.

3. **Careers education is more than just advertising a list of jobs to students.**
   One of the most important themes that has arisen from this book is that there is much more involved in careers education than simply showing students the jobs which we think they would be good at. It is about inspiring, supporting, skilling, and preparing them to be able to find a path through life which is their own. This is always the hardest mentality to shift with teaching and the leadership of staff, but is essential if a careers programme is going to develop out of perfunctory into life-changing. Don't let your staff fall into the trap of assuming careers education is job education. They are two vastly different concepts and needed to be treated as such.

Teacher support is one of the most important aspects of any careers programme that wants to be deep and interwoven. If they are not supported and resourced sufficiently to have the confidence to take risks and step out of their comfort zone, there can be no legacy; it will stall before it starts. In order to sustain something new in their practice, there needs to be trust that it will not be perfect the first time. It takes a leap of faith, in the knowledge they have the backing of the school, that they are not alone. There only needs to be one message that accompanies this: "it's okay to get it wrong, there is no reward without risk". Wait, no, two messages, "it's not about replanning or redesigning, it's about rethinking and reframing". Near enough everything that needs to be done already exists; it is just about taking a chance, having faith in yourself that together we can find it and bring it out.

I sincerely hope that throughout the course of this book that you have been able to find solutions to your particular barriers or avenues of interest. If you're lucky you may have also been able to create a tangible articulation onto systematic issues that you are currently facing. If you're really lucky, I might have introduced some new problems for you to tackle and break down so that you can build a truly unique and meaningful programme of study for your students.

Asking schools to ignore academics is not the purpose of this book. The acquisition of knowledge plays a vital role in education. Without it, we risk losing touch with the history of human achievement. As a result, we may also lose our ability to innovate or to build on the collective wealth of knowledge held by humanity. It cannot, however, be the sole focus of our schools. There is a clear and apparent need for students to enter the world of work with the ability to apply everything they have learnt in all manner of ways. From the interpersonal skills required to contribute to a team, to the analytic and critical processes that are the key to interacting with AI technologies. We need to start looking towards a skills integrated approach where there is a dual focus within school and lessons, the traditional and the forward-looking.

With information being so readily available in the digital age, the attributes that will set your students apart and drive success are the ones which give them the ability to engage with it meaningfully. In such a way that sifts through the fake or misleading headlines and can interrogate intelligent systems in a manner that they enhance their processes, rather than replacing them.

This can never be done in isolation; it has to be contributed to by all that work with the development of young people, from teachers to parents and everything in between. Be it the one-off school trips, the inspirational guest speaker in a Year 8 assembly, the industry visitors during a KS2 STEM week, or a conversation in the car journey home after an enlightening parents' evening. There are so many opportunities for students to prepare for, inspire and engage with their futures, than there ever has been before. As teachers, we are on the front line, delivering life-changing lessons on a daily basis. To provide the best possible opportunities, keep just one question at the front of your mind: "How will a student recall this moment in 5, 10, or 20 years' time?"

Inspiring change in the attitudes and actions of students is hard enough, but if we are going to make their future a brighter one than our past, we have to inspire change from the top, middle, and bottom. We are living in a moment in history where continuing along the path we are currently on is only going to maintain the status quo. This is not sustainable. We must act now, and we must shift the focus of education in such a way that it better prepares them for a future that they cannot yet see for themselves.

Our job as teachers and those working to educate young people is to show them this future that lies ahead of them. Not to scare or intimidate, but to prepare them to be ready for its demands on them. The better prepared, the smoother the transition; the smoother the transition, the greater the chance of finding careers which inspire, empassion, and fulfill them, driving them forward.

On one hand, it is a big ask, yet on the other, it is common sense. Don't prepare students for the careers that you think they would be good at; don't prepare them for the careers that they think they want. Prepare them for life, prepare them for the twists and turns of a dynamic job market, regardless of the career they pursue. They probably won't remember the lesson you taught, but they will hold tight the knowledge and passions you imparted to them. Careers education does not sit alongside the curriculum; it sits inside it. It is woven into its fabric and seeps into every aspect of school life; it is, at the end of the day, what schools are here for.

Careers education is education.

Further reading and additional resources

AI in Education

AI in Education is a collaborative community who are using AI technologies and solutions to enhance teacher practice and delivery. Packed full of case studies reports from its many panels of teachers and leaders from all school sectors, each specialising in a different field with the common goal of supporting teachers in the ethical use of AI.

www.ai-in-education.co.uk

Apprentice Ambassador Network

This is a national network made of a number of regional hubs who are some of the most important and loudest voices to advocate for apprenticeships. They have the capacity to work with students and teachers to raise awareness of this progression path. All it takes is an email or phone call to get the relationship started.

www.apprenticeships.gov.uk/influencers/what-is-the-aan

Career Development Institute

The list detailing everything that the people at the Career Development Institute do would take up the word count allocation I have for this book. Ranging from a register of career professionals to a bank of CDPs that covers every aspect of careers professionalism. To say there is a wealth of knowledge would be an understatement; there is a library of resources to sink a small ocean liner.

www.thecdi.net

Careers and Enterprise Company

Other than providing funding for the numerous careers hubs up and down the country, they provide funding for training, resources, and case studies from primary through to tertiary education. If you are ever short of inspiration or in need of support, this is the place to turn to.

www.careersandenterprise.co.uk

Gatsby Foundation

It might seem obvious, but there is more to them than the eight Gatsby Benchmarks. There is an enormous amount of research and publications ranging from the implementation of the benchmarks through to guidance on the delivery of technical education. If you are in need of evidence to back up what you are trying to do, these are the go-to people.

www.gatsby.org.uk/

Job of the Week

Job of the Week YouTube channel is a comprehensive set of video resources providing spotlights on different jobs, ranging from the well-known to the slightly more obscure or lesser known. These act as an incredible resource when used in conjunction with other aspects of careers delivery with students and staff. Simply showing the existence of different careers can often be enough to spark the fire of discovery inside someone.

www.youtube.com/@mypathcareersuk

Local Skills Improvement Plans

A national strategy to seek out skills sectors in need of development, often contributed by geographically significant Chambers of Commerce with their contribution as well as multiple local businesses. There are regular reports produced that highlight local areas of focus, these often highlight skills or employment sector gaps which they are seeking to fill.

www.gov.uk/government/publications/designated-employer-representative-bodies/notice-of-designated-employer-representative-bodies

Myfuture

Myfuture has been developed by Australia's National Careers Service. While some elements are very specific to the Australian education system, there is a vast amount of universally applicable research and resources available to freely download and use. Ranging from short, digestible reports from their insights section to a wide range of classroom teaching activities.

https://myfuture.com

Springpod

A vast array of student-focused content that provides virtual work experience opportunities for students. Created and delivered in partnership with business and enterprise, there is a course to suit any learner with any interest. Certificates of completion are available and all experience can be added onto students' CVs.

www.springpod.com

Start Small; Dream Big

A pilot programme for primary schools was developed by the Careers and Enterprise Company in 2022. Evidence-backed and published reports from initial trials, this website provides resources and documentation to help school leaders implement a careers programme in their schools.

www.careersandenterprise.co.uk/news/you-re-never-too-young-to-dream-big

STEM Learning

STEM Learning, as an organisation has an array of resources available to educators, ranging from lesson plans and activities through to connecting teachers with employers to support with STEM-related activities. With the ever-increasing focus on making the UK a beacon for science and innovation, STEM learning is paving the way to bring it into the schools.

www.stem.org.uk

World Economic Forum

The annual report "Future of Jobs" evaluates current employment and workforce trends and highlights the industries in high-growth demand and those on the wane. In addition to this, it also includes the skills that are going to be most sought after by employers and their related industry sectors.

www.weforum.org

NEW AND BESTSELLING FROM TROTMAN

New in 2025

Getting Into University

Careers Essentials

Estd. 1969

Enhance your careers library with our bestsellers, visit: www.trotman.co.uk